Christian Heroes: Then & Now

JONATHAN GOFORTH

An Open Door in China

Christian Heroes: Then & Now

JONATHAN GOFORTH

An Open Door in China

JANET & GEOFF BENGE

YWAM Publishing
Seattle, Washington

YWAM Publishing is the publishing ministry of Youth With A Mission (YWAM), an international missionary organization of Christians from many denominations dedicated to presenting Jesus Christ to this generation. To this end, YWAM has focused its efforts in three main areas: (1) training and equipping believers for their part in fulfilling the Great Commission (Matthew 28:19), (2) personal evangelism, and (3) mercy ministry (medical and relief work).

For a free catalog of books and materials, call (425) 771-1153 or (800) 922-2143. Visit us online at www.ywampublishing.com.

Jonathan Goforth: An Open Door in China

Published by YWAM Publishing
a ministry of Youth With A Mission
P.O. Box 55787, Seattle, WA 98155-0787

Publisher's Cataloging-in-Publication *(Provided by Quality Books, Inc.)*
Benge, Janet, 1958-
Jonathan Goforth : an open door in China / Janet & Geoff Benge. —1st ed.
p. cm — (Christian heroes, then & now)
Includes bibliographical references.
ISBN-10: 1-57658-174-8
1. Goforth, Jonathan, 1859-1936. 2. Missionaries—China—Biography. 3. Missionaries—Canada—Biography. 4. Missions—China. I. Benge, Geoff, 1954- II. Title. III. Series.
BV3427.G6B46 2000 266'.0092 QBI00-809

ISBN 978-1-57658-174-2 (paperback)
ISBN 978-1-57658-571-9 (e-book)

Sixth printing 2020

Printed in the United States of America

Christian Heroes: Then & Now

Adoniram Judson
Amy Carmichael
Betty Greene
Brother Andrew
Cameron Townsend
Charles Mulli
Clarence Jones
Corrie ten Boom
Count Zinzendorf
C. S. Lewis
C. T. Studd
David Bussau
David Livingstone
Dietrich Bonhoeffer
D. L. Moody
Elisabeth Elliot
Eric Liddell
Florence Young
Francis Asbury
George Müller
Gladys Aylward
Helen Roseveare
Hudson Taylor
Ida Scudder
Isobel Kuhn
Jacob DeShazer
Jim Elliot
John Flynn
John Newton
John Wesley
John Williams
Jonathan Goforth
Klaus-Dieter John
Lillian Trasher
Loren Cunningham
Lottie Moon
Mary Slessor
Mildred Cable
Nate Saint
Norman Grubb
Paul Brand
Rachel Saint
Richard Wurmbrand
Rowland Bingham
Samuel Zwemer
Sundar Singh
Wilfred Grenfell
William Booth
William Carey

Available in paperback, e-book, and audiobook formats.Unit study curriculum guides are available for select biographies.

www.HeroesThenAndNow.com

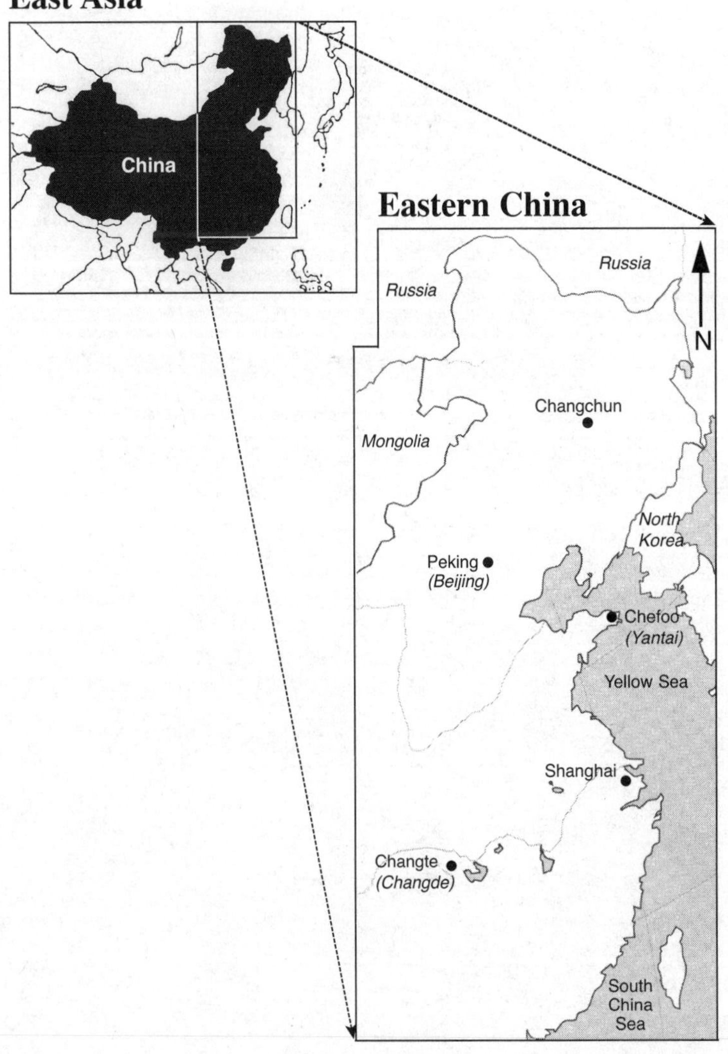
East Asia
China
Eastern China
Russia
Russia
N
Changchun
Mongolia
North Korea
Peking
(Beijing)
Chefoo
(Yantai)
Yellow Sea
Shanghai
Changte
(Changde)
South China Sea

Contents

Chapter 1

Twice Saved

Five-year-old Jonathan Goforth climbed proudly onto the wagon. He was about to accompany his uncle Tom to the market, where his uncle would sell the grain Jonathan's father had painstakingly coaxed to grow during a particularly dry summer.

"You can't sit there, lad. The slightest jolt and you'll be sliding off the wagon," said Uncle Tom as Jonathan was about to sit down and make himself comfortable on some sacks of grain. "Here, I'll move a couple of these sacks aside, and you can nestle down in the hollow between them. You'll be as safe as a tick in a blanket there," he continued with a twinkle in his eye.

Jonathan snuggled down securely into the hollow his uncle had created for him, and with a crack of the reins they were off. The two old draft horses pulling the wagon ambled along through the countryside on the five-mile trip to London, Ontario, where the market was located. From his vantage point on the wagon, Jonathan could see farmers out in their fields harvesting wheat and corn.

As the wagon rolled along the dirt road, the horses picked up speed until they almost broke into a run as they descended a slope in the road. The wheels rattled over the rutted road. Suddenly the wagon lurched sharply to the right. Jonathan heard his uncle yell for him to hold on, but it was too late. In the split second it took for the wheels of the wagon to slip into a particularly deep rut, he was pitched from his safe spot between the sacks of grain and was flying through the air. He landed with a thud on the ground beneath the wagon. Searing pain shot up his right side. As he gasped for air, Jonathan noticed to his horror that the back wheel of the loaded wagon was about to roll over him. At the same instant, he felt his uncle's large hand reach down and grab the back of his shirt. With a jerk of his powerful arm, Uncle Tom pulled Jonathan out of the path of the wheel just before it rolled over the spot where he was lying. As his uncle hauled him back onto the wagon, Jonathan felt his shirt rip in two. He didn't care; he was alive, and a shirt could be mended.

It took several minutes for Uncle Tom to regain control of the frightened horses and bring the wagon to a halt. "Are you all right, lad?" he asked when he had finally done so.

Jonathan nodded slowly, too shocked to speak.

"It was a close call," his uncle went on, ruffling Jonathan's sandy blond hair. "Your shirt is a bit the worse for wear. Still we must be on our way to the market."

Uncle Tom reset the two sacks, and Jonathan snuggled back into the hollow between them. For the rest of the journey, though, he held tightly on to the corners of the sacks.

Later that night back at the farm as the family gathered round to hear news from London, Uncle Tom recounted the story of how the wagon wheels had gotten caught in a deep rut and had flung Jonathan into the path of the back wheel. Jonathan watched his mother's eyes widen as she listened.

"Do you hurt anywhere?" Jane Goforth finally asked in her lilting Irish accent.

Jonathan shook his head. "No, Ma," he replied. "But I did rip my shirt."

"That's easily fixed," she said, smiling down at her seventh child.

Jonathan smiled back. Of all the useful things his mother could do, the thing she prided herself on the most was her ability to make and mend clothes for her husband and eleven children. Indeed, Jonathan often heard his father say she was the best seamstress in all Canada. In a couple of days his shirt would be as good as new.

The next day, Jonathan had a large bruise on his right hip from the fall, and his father gave him a day off from farmwork. Jonathan stayed at home and helped his mother make soap. He and his brothers all took turns doing "women's work" around the house, since there were ten boys in the family and only one girl.

After the beef fat had been cut up into cubes and placed in a large copper pot on the stove to be boiled down to tallow to make the soap, Jonathan's mother beckoned for him to sit beside her at the table. She pulled down the family Bible from a shelf and opened it. "I think you're up to Psalm 78," she said to her son.

Jonathan began to read from the old Bible. "'Give ear, O my people, to my law: incline your ears to the words of my mouth. I will open my mouth in a parable: I will utter dark sayings of old.'" He read the entire psalm—all seventy-two verses—to his mother.

When he had finished reading, his mother hugged him. "You did a fine job, son," she said.

Jonathan felt his chest puff out with pride. He was only five years old, and though he hadn't started school yet, he could already read! He had learned through listening to his older brothers reciting their lessons after dinner each night.

"Next month is October, and you'll be going to school with the big children," said his mother.

Jonathan nodded. "But I'll still read the Bible to you, no matter how much reciting I have to do at school," he said.

Reading the Psalms and going to church on Sunday with his mother were the only religious activities Jonathan knew about. Jonathan's father, Francis, was a hardworking farmer who had migrated from

Yorkshire, England, with his father and two brothers. He had been only a teenager then, but by sheer hard work and willpower, now, twenty years later, he owned two productive farms. Working from dawn till dusk, though, left him with little time to think about religion. He never even said grace before a meal or prayed with the children at night. If it weren't for his mother's simple faith, Jonathan would have grown up knowing very little about God.

Jonathan did go to school, though not until November, when his father could spare the boys from the farm. Some aspects of school disappointed Jonathan. It felt to him like he was going to have to wait forever for the other five-year-olds in the class to catch up to his reading level. However, there was one thing he loved from the very first day. Beside the chalkboard was a map, which captured Jonathan's attention. After class was dismissed for recess, he would stand in front of the map and study it. First he would find London, Ontario, the nearest big town, and then he would stand back and look at the whole world, trying hard to imagine what it was like in the other places named on the map.

The idea that millions of other people lived in these far-off places boggled Jonathan's mind. The young boy was determined to learn all he could about these foreign locations. Indeed, he studied hard and was always near the top of his class.

Life in the Goforth home followed the pattern of the seasons. In June, when school was out for the summer, Jonathan and his brothers would help their father harvest the family's crops. If they managed to get the job done early, Mr. Goforth would then often hire out his older sons to neighboring farms to help with the harvest. Most winters the children got to attend school, but when money was in short supply, they didn't. During those years, the money normally spent on schooling was needed to buy fabric for clothing and extra provisions for the long, hard Canadian winter.

Everyone in the Goforth home, from the oldest to the youngest, was expected to pull his or her weight. It was no surprise to anyone when, in the spring of his fifteenth year as Jonathan finished elementary school, his father put him in charge of the family's second farm called Thamesford Farm. The farm was located about twenty miles from the family's main farm near Thorndale. Jonathan took over running the farm just in time to plant the seed for the summer crops. First, though, he had to get rid of all the weeds that had sprung up since the last harvest. This was a backbreaking job. The fields had to be plowed and then plowed again, exposing the roots of the weeds to the sun long enough to dry them out and kill them. Once this was done, the seed was sown by hand. And once the seeds turned into tiny seedlings, it was Jonathan's job to nurse them along until they were tall, strong stands of wheat.

Although taking care of the farm took up most of Jonathan's time that summer, like many other young men in the area, he made time to help a neighbor build a barn. Every person in the community helped at such times because they knew that one day it might be themselves needing help with a new barn. It was virtually impossible for one person to erect a barn alone.

While the men pulled solid beams of wood into place and hammered away, the women busied themselves preparing huge pots of stew for the men to eat at lunchtime. By midafternoon, the sides of the barn were up, and it was time to raise the roof beams into place. This task involved using ropes to lift the enormous timbers up and then maneuvering them into position, straddling the outside wall of the barn and the center ridgepole. Jonathan was on the floor in the middle of the barn pulling on one of the ropes when he heard a woman yell, "Look out! The beams are giving way!"

Jonathan jerked his head upward just in time to see the beams above him slam into one another and begin to fall. His first urge was to sprint the ten feet to safety, but there was no time. Yet the falling beams would kill him if he didn't do something. In an instant he made a decision: Instead of running, he would stay where he was and try his best to dodge the falling beams. Keeping his eyes skyward, Jonathan watched the beams whoosh past him and thump onto the ground. With each beam that came tumbling down, he would dart to the left or the right to avoid it. Seconds later, all of the beams had fallen, and Jonathan was still standing! For the second time in his life, Jonathan Goforth had cheated death.

After this experience, Jonathan spent a lot of time thinking about what he should do with his twice-saved life. Finally he came to the conclusion that he should be a politician. During his time at Thamesford Farm, he had often walked into Wyton, the nearest town, to attend political meetings. He had become convinced that being in government was the way to bring real change to Canada.

Most nights after his chores on the farm were done, Jonathan would stroll down to the edge of a swamp on the farm. He would take his place atop a mound of dirt and practice giving speeches. He would imagine there were hundreds of people in front of him hanging on every word he said and cheering when they heard how he would improve their lives and do something about the plight of farmers. He yelled at the top of his lungs. Often, when he went into London to sell butter at the market, men would joke with Jonathan about hearing him from the highway that passed a mile to the east of the swamp!

Jonathan talked to his father about his new career plans. Although Jonathan had done a wonderful job with Thamesford Farm, Mr. Goforth could see that his son's heart was not in farming. He agreed to send Jonathan to London, Ontario, to attend a short commercial course. This type of training, Jonathan hoped, would provide a good background for a politician.

When he got to London, Jonathan worked hard and did well in the course. When it was over, to

Jonathan's surprise, the teacher suggested he go back and finish high school. The nearest high school to the family farm was located in Ingersoll, close to where Jonathan's brother Will and his wife now lived. Jonathan knew he would be welcome to stay with them while he attended school. Still, he struggled with taking what to him seemed like a backwards step. In the end, though, he decided to follow the teacher's advice. It was a decision that would change the course of his life and ultimately take him halfway around the world.

A visiting teacher, the Reverend Mr. Lachlan Cameron, had a great effect on Jonathan while he was in high school. Mr. Cameron visited the school regularly to instruct the students in Bible study. However, it wasn't so much what Mr. Cameron said that impressed seventeen-year-old Jonathan as it was his kind manner. The two of them became friends, and Jonathan decided the polite thing for him to do was to visit the Reverend Mr. Cameron's Presbyterian church to hear him preach.

It was quite a walk to the church from his brother Will's house, but Jonathan made the trek anyway, first one Sunday, and then the next, and the Sunday after that. On Jonathan's third visit, the Reverend Mr. Cameron, as he always did at the end of each sermon, invited those who wanted to become Christians to bow their heads and pray. Throughout the sermon, Jonathan had been struggling with the idea of following God, and by the end of the service, he had settled the matter in his heart. Right there, as Mr. Cameron had suggested, Jonathan prayed a simple, quiet prayer giving his life to God.

That week when Mr. Cameron came to school, Jonathan told him what had happened. Mr. Cameron was delighted and offered to let Jonathan teach Sunday school, which Jonathan eagerly agreed to do. Jonathan soon found the Bible interesting and alive, and he wanted to share the wisdom of what he read in its pages with all those around him.

Soon after Jonathan became a Christian, his parents came to stay at his brother Will's house for a month. Jonathan saw this as a wonderful opportunity to tell his parents about his new faith. He decided they should all have family devotions together and that he should lead them. Though he had no idea how his father would react to this suggestion, when his sister-in-law had cleared the dishes from the table the first night, Jonathan cleared his throat and said, "We're going to have family devotions tonight, so please don't leave."

Much to his surprise, they all stayed exactly where they were. Jonathan had his Bible ready on the sideboard, and he opened it and read a chapter from the Book of Isaiah. He made a few comments about what the chapter meant and then invited his family to kneel and pray with him. They all did that night and every night that his parents were there.

It was a good thing that Jonathan's new faith was accepted at home, because it wasn't at school. Jonathan's teacher embraced the ideas of Thomas

Paine. After the American Revolution, Paine had written a pamphlet called *The Age of Reason,* which criticized Christianity for being outdated and irrelevant to modern society.

All the students in the class followed the teacher's lead, making fun of Jonathan and mocking his simple beliefs. Jonathan withstood their taunts as long as he could, but after a while he grew tired of their sarcastic remarks. Yet he didn't know what to do. He had no answers for Thomas Paine's criticism of Christianity. Slowly he felt his new faith begin to crumble. Finally he decided the Bible must have the answers he needed; he just had to dig deeper to find them. Every night for many weeks, when he had finished his farm chores, Jonathan would sit down with his Bible and look for answers. And he found them. By the time school recessed for summer, Jonathan's faith was much stronger. Not only that, he had found convincing ways to answer the questions and taunts hurled against him. First his teacher and then his fellow students gave up their "sophisticated" beliefs and became Christians.

Jonathan was amazed. Right there and then he decided to become a Presbyterian pastor instead of a politician. He spoke to the Reverend Mr. Cameron about his desire. Mr. Cameron was delighted by Jonathan's decision and began to tutor him in Latin and Greek in preparation for attending Knox College in Toronto, where Jonathan would train to be a pastor.

Jonathan also began sending away for bulk orders of tracts and gave them to everyone he knew, even the elderly women at church. The women were amused to be a part of his evangelistic efforts.

Not long after this, Jonathan was invited to a meeting held by an elderly missionary to Formosa (now Taiwan). Jonathan sat spellbound as Dr. Mackay preached a lively sermon. Towards the end of the presentation, the old missionary's voice grew quiet. "For the past two years," he said, "I have traveled from one end of Canada to the other trying to interest some young man in following me back to Formosa. But I have not been able to find a single man. It seems no one has caught the vision. I am getting ready to go back alone. I have no doubt that soon my bones will be lying in a grave on some Formosan hillside. That is no tragedy. To me the tragedy is that no young man has heard the call to come and carry on the work that I have begun."

As Jonathan listened to Dr. Mackay utter these words, he felt overwhelmed with shame. He wished the floor would open up and swallow him. Wasn't he a young man? Why had he assumed he should become a pastor, having to travel no farther away from home than Toronto? A Bible verse came to mind. It was from Isaiah chapter six, verse eight, which he had read many times: "Whom shall I send, and who will go for us?" In an instant, Jonathan knew why his life had been spared twice. He was called to be a missionary, to go to some unknown place where the gospel had never been heard before.

The idea gripped Jonathan's heart, and he began to read every book and article he could find about foreign missions. He had four years of training at Knox College ahead of him, but he was convinced that when he graduated, he would be on his way to serve in some far-off place, as distant as any he had studied on the classroom map back in elementary school.

Chapter 2

A Country Bumpkin

It was October 1883, and Jonathan Goforth stood waiting for the train. He had a huge grin on his face. He could hardly believe that at twenty-four years of age he was finally on his way to Knox College, one hundred twenty miles away in Toronto. At first he had been a little nervous about going. After all, he'd never been in a big city before. For the first time in his life he would be surrounded by strangers. He calmed his nerves by reminding himself that even though his fellow students at Knox College might start out as strangers, they would soon be friends, since they had so much in common. All twenty-three of the students who would make up his class were training to become Presbyterian pastors or missionaries. Jonathan could scarcely imagine what it was going to be like with so many other enthusiastic and dedicated young men around. He thought of the Bible studies they would have together and the prayer meetings. It was almost too good to be true.

As the train rounded a bend and approached the station, Jonathan hugged his mother good-bye. "Thank you for everything, Ma," he said, emotion suddenly choking his voice.

"Mind you don't get that new suit of yours dirty before you even get to the city," replied his mother.

Jonathan could hear the pride in her voice—pride that he was going off to college and pride for the new suit and shirt he was wearing. She had sat up late many nights hand sewing them. She told Jonathan he needed to look his best, since he was the first Goforth to go off to college.

"I'll take good care of it, Ma," he said as the train puffed its way to a halt beside the tiny station platform. "This suit has to last me four years, and then some!"

Jonathan swung his suitcase onto the train, and after a hurried farewell to his father and the five of his brothers who had come to see him off, he climbed aboard, found a seat, and waved good-bye.

"God bless you, lad," yelled his father as the locomotive lunged forward and the train began to pull away from the station.

The remark brought tears to Jonathan's eyes. Two years earlier, soon after Jonathan had decided to become a missionary, his father had become a

Christian. Now he stood waving enthusiastically as his son set off for a Christian college. Not only that, but he had promised to support Jonathan's plans in any way he could.

The trip to Toronto was almost like a dream. Jonathan had never been so far away from home. There were so many new sights and sounds to take in as the train rattled along through the rolling green Ontario countryside. Finally Jonathan arrived at Knox College, an imposing old stone building, where he was confident he would spend four happy and productive years studying.

Upon arrival at Knox College, Jonathan got straight down to business. He feared that with twenty-two other eager students in his class, all of the opportunities for Christian service would soon be taken. So he asked one of the college professors for directions to the poorest part of the city. The professor directed him to an area called the Ward, located south of the college. Jonathan would have liked to have asked one of the other students to go with him, but since he didn't know any of them yet, he went to the Ward alone.

It was early evening as Jonathan strolled the streets of the Ward slum district. He prayed as he walked, and to his amazement many young women came right up to talk to him. Many of them offered to spend time with him. At first their reaction puzzled Jonathan, who finally decided it was because his prayers were working. The young women, it seemed, were somehow drawn to him to learn more about the gospel. Encouraged by the "openness" of people in the area, Jonathan walked for several miles through the streets developing a plan to visit every home in the area and to spend time talking to and praying with as many of the young women as he could.

By the time Jonathan got back to Knox College later that night, he was excited by all the possibilities that lay ahead of him in the Ward. In fact, he was so excited about ministering in the Ward district that that was all he talked about at dinner the following evening. The students ate together, and whenever there was a lull in the conversation, Jonathan cleared his throat and began to speak. "I don't know if any of you have had the chance to get down to the slum area yet, but I went last night and I was astounded by the openness there to the gospel."

Most of the other students stopped eating and listened intently. "What do you mean?" asked one of the young men.

"Well," replied Jonathan, enthusiastically, "take the young women, for example. I must have had ten or fifteen come right up to me and ask me what they could do for me! At home the young ladies are shy, but in the Ward they are very forward. I think God must have been working in their hearts, don't you?"

At first Jonathan saw a couple of the students cover their mouths with their hands, and then he heard a snicker or two. Within a minute the entire room had erupted into loud howls of laughter.

Jonathan felt the prickly sensation of his ears and cheeks turning hot and red. What had he said that was so funny? He had no idea.

When the laughter finally died down, the student to his right elbowed him. "Haven't you ever seen a prostitute before?" he smirked.

"Didn't you wonder why those girls were so friendly?" taunted another student.

"You're joking, aren't you, Jonathan?" questioned a third.

"No! I think he's telling the truth," blurted the young man who sat next to Jonathan at morning devotions. "Look at the country boy's clothes! Ha, Jonathan! Did your mama make them for you?"

Jonathan sat in stunned silence, unable to reply to anything the students had said to him, unable to imagine that this was the response of students in a Christian college. For the first time he studied the clothes the other students were wearing. Every one of them had on a fancy city suit. Jonathan wondered how he had been so stupid not to notice before now.

Eventually the taunting died down and the dinner conversation moved on to other things, but Jonathan was not interested in taking part. All he wanted to do was to get away to his room and be alone.

Later that night, after he had thought about the incident at dinner, Jonathan knew he would never fit in until he had city clothes like the other students. He had a small amount of money that was supposed to keep him for the first semester, and he decided to spend some of it on having a new suit made. He promised himself he would never let his mother know what he'd done. She would be very upset to learn that her loving handiwork had made her son the laughingstock of the college.

The following day when class was out, Jonathan did not go to the Ward. Instead he went into town and bought five yards of medium-quality black suiting fabric. He planned to take the fabric to a tailor the following evening and have a suit made. However, something happened that night—something worse than Jonathan had ever experienced in his life—that prevented him from doing so.

After dinner that night, Jonathan went upstairs to study. He was sitting alone in his room with his back to the door when he heard it open. He turned to see who it was, and much to his surprise, all of the first-year students were crowding into his room. Jonathan was puzzled; he couldn't think of any reason for a mass visit at this time of night. Suddenly he saw the length of rope one of the students was carrying, and his blood froze. He searched the faces of his fellow students and saw hatred and disdain. "What do you want?" he asked as evenly as he could.

"A bit of fun with a country bumpkin!" laughed the student holding the rope. "Hold him down, boys!"

Jonathan felt the bite of the rope against his wrists as it was tied around them, and then on around his body. He tried desperately not to panic, even though he had no idea what was going to happen next.

"What's this?" yelled a student.

Looking towards his bed, Jonathan saw that the student was holding up the length of fabric he had bought earlier in the day.

"Going to get a new look, were you?" said the student. "Well, let's get you into that new look right now!"

Another student, the tallest in the group, jeered. "Yeah, maybe we can dandy you up so you can go and visit those girls in the Ward again."

Everyone laughed.

Jonathan watched in horror as a pair of scissors were produced and someone hacked a large hole in the center of the piece of fabric. The student who had cut the hole then pulled the fabric over Jonathan's head and wound it tightly around his body until he looked like a mummy in black.

The next thing he knew, Jonathan was lifted into the air and carried out into the corridor. The students lined up along the wall as Jonathan was deposited at the far end. "Get back to your room if you can!" screamed one of the young men, kicking Jonathan to start him moving down the corridor lined with students.

Jonathan was so tightly bound he could only hobble, but he could see that no one was going to let him alone until he reached the other end of the hall. So he set out on the nightmare thirty-foot journey back to his room. Along the way the students taunted and jeered and pushed him. Somehow, though, he got to the other end, but to his dismay, he was turned around and sent back down the line. It was half an hour before the students were finished with their "fun" with Jonathan and he was allowed to return to his room. Someone unwound him and loosened the rope, and then he was left alone. He could hear the laughter of the other students recede down the corridor as they returned to their rooms.

When he had finally untangled himself from the rope and fabric, Jonathan fell onto his bed. His whole body shook with deep sobs. His hopes were as crumpled as the length of suit fabric that now lay on the floor. He had wanted so much to be a part of the college, to be friends with the other students, to pray and learn with them, but now he knew that he was alone. How stupid he had been to think that all that separated him from the others was a fancy new suit! He would always be a simple country boy, and the other students would never let him forget it. He had no one to comfort him. He could never tell his parents what had happened; they would be appalled and probably make him return home. No, Jonathan knew he had a lonely path ahead of him—four years of taunting and ridicule before he had the qualifications he needed to reach his goal. In deep despair he slipped to his knees and reached for the only thing he knew could bring him comfort—his Bible.

Although he was deeply hurt by the actions of his fellow students, Jonathan had set his sights on a goal, and he would not give up. A few days after his humiliation by the other students, he joined the William Street Mission and became one of its most successful workers. His work took him not only to the streets of the Ward but also to Don jail. At first the warden would only allow him to stand in the assembly hall and yell down the corridor. Although Jonathan could not see any of the prisoners, he was certain they were listening to him as he preached to them week after week. Eventually the warden came to trust Jonathan and one day allowed him down the corridor into the cellblock. Jonathan was very happy about this. Now he could see face-to-face the prisoners he had been preaching to. The prisoners were not so happy to see Jonathan, though. One of them growled, "Go away. You're wasting your time! I don't even believe there is a God."

The rest of the prisoners cheered their vocal comrade on. Thinking quickly, Jonathan waited for the noise to die down and then replied to the prisoner, "Well, my good friend, it's strange you should say that, because the book I am holding talks about you."

"Ha," scoffed the prisoner. "What does it say?"

Jonathan turned to Psalm 14 and began reading: "'The fool has said in his heart there is no God.'"

The prisoner was silent. Sensing an opportunity, Jonathan spoke for about twenty minutes on the verse. By the time he was finished, a number of the prisoners were weeping openly. Jonathan went from cell to cell talking to the prisoners, many of whom begged him to tell them how to become a Christian. Jonathan went away very encouraged, promising to return and talk to the prisoners again the following week.

Once back at Knox College, he was bursting to tell someone the good news from the prison. He chose to tell one of the three students who had come and apologized for the way they had humiliated him during the first week. This time as he shared, his fellow student did not mock. In fact, he seemed as pleased as Jonathan at the turn of events. Jonathan allowed himself a moment of hope, hope that one day he would feel part of the college after all.

Meanwhile, Jonathan made it his goal to visit every home in the Ward slum, even though there were thousands of them. His plan was simple. He would knock on a door, and when someone opened the door a crack to see who was there, he would stick his foot into the doorway so that the door could not be shut. Then Jonathan would ask the person if he could come in and talk with him or her about Christian matters. He was turned down only twice in his four years at college. His success and his fearlessness in venturing into areas filled with criminals and misfits slowly won him the respect of his classmates.

After a few visits to the Ward, Jonathan befriended a local policeman. "How do you have the courage to go into those alleyways? My fellow officers and I never go there unless we are in groups of two or three!"

"I never go in alone either," replied Jonathan, chuckling. "I always take someone with me too: God!"

A year later, Jonathan needed to remind himself of this fact. There were many times when he was scheduled by Knox College to speak at outlying churches. When he didn't have the money to pay for a train fare to get to these locations, he walked to them. One spring morning on his way to speak in a church, he took a shortcut through some thick woods. As he rounded a corner on the trail, he froze in his steps. There in front of him was an enormous black bear. The bear stood up tall, its long claws glinting in the morning sunlight, before settling back on its haunches. Jonathan knew it was useless to run; a bear could easily outrun a man. As he wondered what to do, the thought came to him: *I am not alone. God is with me, and I am about His business. He will protect me.*

With that, Jonathan began to edge slowly and smoothly forward. He could feel the bear's fur as he inched past the animal. He kept his eyes looking frontward and his steps as steady as he could. The bear stood completely still, as if stuck to the path. Jonathan never looked back, and the bear never followed him. Later when he wrote to his parents about the incident, he imagined it would be the most dangerous situation he would ever find himself in. He was wrong, very wrong, about that.

Chapter 3

You Go to China, We'll Supply the Money

No one was more surprised than Jonathan that within a year of beginning at Knox College he had gone from being the butt of everyone's jokes to one of the most popular students in the class. One by one, all the students in his class had sought Jonathan out and apologized for the way they had treated him during the first week of college. They confided that they had expected him to go home after their merciless humiliation of him. The fact that he had not only stayed on at Knox College but also been kind and courteous to them had made them ashamed of their behavior. Their attitude changed so much that when Jonathan shared with them about his ministry in the slums, they marveled at his bravery and waited eagerly to hear each new report about his work. Donald McGillivray, the top language student in the class, became Jonathan's closest friend. He often helped Jonathan with his Greek and Hebrew studies, which were his weakest subjects.

By the end of their second year at Knox College, many of the students gathered in Jonathan's room on Friday nights. Earlier in the year Jonathan had purchased ten copies of a booklet titled *China's Spiritual Needs and Claims,* written by the famous English missionary Hudson Taylor. Jonathan had sent copies of the booklet to a number of local pastors asking them to take the time to read it. Soon he found other books and leaflets that discussed the spiritual needs of people in China. Before Jonathan knew it, the floor of his room was stacked with books waiting to be sent off to pastors. He had continued to do this for months, as finances would allow, and slowly news of what he was doing spread. Christians started sending him money so that he could send the challenging books to pastors all over Canada. It soon became an overwhelming task to wrap, address, and mail all the books. As a result, a group of Jonathan's classmates stepped in to help each Friday night.

The first thing Jonathan would do when they got together on Friday nights was read aloud the letters he had received during the week. Then they would total up the cash donations that came with the letters and see how many books they could afford to mail out that week. After a prayer thanking God for the letters and money and asking Him to bless the people who received the books, they set to work wrapping and addressing parcels of books.

On Saturdays Jonathan would study and prepare sermons to preach at the churches in his home mission field—an area on the outskirts of Toronto twenty-two miles long by twelve miles wide over which his professors at Knox College had given him responsibility. Jonathan took his home mission field duties seriously. As he had done in the Ward slum, he challenged himself to visit every house in the area. At each door he introduced himself and invited the people to come to hear him preach at one of the local churches on Sunday.

Most people had never had a preacher personally invite them to church before. So many responded that the churches where Jonathan spoke were soon overflowing with people. When the pews were all filled, people would stand at the back and in the aisles; some even found places to sit and stand around the pulpit. But no matter how crowded it got, Jonathan never complained. He was delighted to have so many people come to hear him preach the gospel.

When Jonathan wanted to make an important point during a sermon, he would fling his arms backwards. On one occasion as he did this, he managed to swipe several of the people crowded in behind the pulpit to hear him. The congregation roared with laughter. They had never seen a pastor hit members of the congregation!

All of this preaching, along with studying about China, convinced Jonathan more than ever that he wanted to be a missionary. In particular, he wanted to be a missionary to China. He could think of no other place on earth where so many people had never had the opportunity to hear the gospel, and he was determined to do something about it. Jonathan had two more years left at Knox College, and during that time he would keep his eyes and ears open for the right opportunity to serve in China.

Every now and then, the thought crossed Jonathan's mind that he should find a wife to go with him to China. He was much too busy, though, to do anything more than think about it. However, during his third year at Knox College, he met Rosalind Bell-Smith. Jonathan was returning home with a large group of students who had all been visiting the Niagara-on-the-Lake Bible Conference. On board the boat as it was crossing Lake Ontario was a group of artists who had been on a picnic to the far shore of the lake.

Jonathan was chatting with Donald McGillivray when he noticed Mr. O'Brien, his friend from the Toronto Mission Union, engaged in a serious conversation with a young woman from the group of artists. The woman nodded and smiled as they spoke, and it was obvious to Jonathan from her actions that she and Mr. O'Brien knew each other. As the conversation seemed to be winding down, Mr. O'Brien spotted Jonathan and called to him. "Over here, Jonathan. I have someone I want you to meet."

Jonathan excused himself from the conversation with Donald McGillivray. As he walked over to where Mr. O'Brien and the well-dressed young woman were seated, he was conscious of his shabby suit and worn shoes. Mr. O'Brien smiled at him.

"Mr. Goforth, I would like you to meet Miss Rosalind Bell-Smith. She played the organ for me at church last Sunday." Then turning to Rosalind he said, "And I should like you to meet Jonathan Goforth, one of our key workers at the Toronto Mission Union."

"I'm pleased to make your acquaintance," said Jonathan, extending his hand to Rosalind Bell-Smith and looking into her determined eyes.

Rosalind shook Jonathan's hand and gave him a broad smile that seemed to animate every square inch of her face.

"Miss Bell-Smith has agreed to join us at the mission next Saturday night and play the organ for us," beamed Mr. O'Brien.

"How good of you," replied Jonathan, noticing as he spoke that the boat was pulling up to the dock.

The following Saturday night Rosalind Bell-Smith sat at the organ. Jonathan was impressed with how well she played. He was also conscious that his eyes kept drifting her way as he preached the sermon.

Later that night, the mission held a meeting, and Rosalind was invited to become a part of a committee being set up to open a new mission on the east side of town. She hesitated for some time before agreeing to join the committee. Jonathan found this odd, and it was a long time before he learned why she had hesitated.

It turned out that Rosalind was a very talented young artist who came from a well-known family. Her father had been Professor John Bell-Smith, the most famous artist in Canada. He had immigrated to Canada from England when Rosalind was three years old and quickly won the position of president of the Canadian Academy of Art. He had groomed Rosalind to follow in his footsteps. He had died the year before, however, when Rosalind was twenty years old, but not before he had insisted his wife make him a solemn promise. The promise was that no matter what happened, after Rosalind graduated from the Toronto Art School, she was to be sent "home" to England for further training at the Kensington School of Art.

When she was asked to join the committee at the Toronto Mission Union, Rosalind had already begun packing for the trip to England to fulfill the promise her mother had made. She knew it would cause a great deal of strife in the family if she announced she wanted to delay the trip. Still, as she hesitated over the decision, something inside her told her she should agree to become part of the committee. She did, and Jonathan felt strangely lightheaded about her decision.

Over the course of the next year, Jonathan and Rosalind worked together at the mission most weekends. By the time October 1886 rolled around, Jonathan was sure he was in love with Rosalind. However, he knew that in asking her to marry him he would be asking her to sign on for a life of hardship and challenge beyond anything that she had encountered during her sheltered and privileged upbringing. Undeterred, Jonathan rehearsed his proposal many times, and one beautiful fall evening he finally decided it was time to ask Rosalind to marry him. "Rosalind," he said quietly, "will you join your life with mine for China?"

Rosalind's eyes shone brightly as she replied, "Oh, Jonathan, of course I will."

Jonathan's heart skipped a beat at her answer. He had worked with Rosalind long enough to know she was as hardworking and dedicated as he was. Still, there was one more thing he needed to ask her. "Would you mind if I did not buy you an engagement ring? It's just that I've ordered a hundred more of Hudson Taylor's booklets, and the postage is going to be high. I'm going to need every penny if I'm to have them all in the mail by Christmas."

Jonathan held his breath while he waited to hear his new fiancée's reply. Would she rather have a ring, or did she want to play a part in challenging fellow Canadians with the spiritual needs of China? He knew it wasn't an easy thing he was asking of her. After all, she had grown up in a much wealthier home than his and had never wanted for anything. Rosalind gulped, and then looking Jonathan straight in the eye she said, "I agreed to join my life with yours for China. What better way to begin?"

Jonathan reached out and held Rosalind's hand, grateful to know he had found a partner who understood what being a missionary was all about.

Not everything went smoothly, however, for twenty-two-year-old Rosalind when she told her mother. Mrs. Bell-Smith was devastated by the news. She had made a solemn oath to her late husband to send Rosalind to England, and she had no intention of breaking the promise. She was adamant that Rosalind set sail for England immediately. And if Rosalind refused to obey her, she would be ordered to leave the house and never return. Rosalind's heart belonged to Jonathan and China, and so with great sorrow, she packed up her things and moved into her brother's home.

The next few months were very difficult for Rosalind. At first her mother would not even speak to her, but slowly she began to soften and eventually apologized, inviting Rosalind to move back home.

While this was going on, Jonathan continued his hectic life. Finally, in his last year at college, he began to turn his attention to how he was going to get to China. He had known when he entered Knox College that the Presbyterian Church had no mission stations in China. Although he'd hoped that some would open up while he was studying, none had, and so Jonathan decided to apply to Hudson Taylor's China Inland Mission. Jonathan had just sent off his application to the mission's headquarters in London, England, when a group of fellow students asked him to meet them in the library.

As he strolled across the quadrangle towards the library, Jonathan wondered what the meeting could be about. He didn't have the slightest idea. As he entered the library, a cheer went up, and Jonathan was surrounded by his entire graduating class.

"Jonathan," announced the class president, "we know that you want to go to China, and we think you should go with the Presbyterian Church."

Jonathan opened his mouth to interrupt, but the president held up his hand and continued. "Of course, we all know the church has no work in China, at present that is, but we have all met together and decided we want to sponsor you as our missionary. We know that no class from Knox College has ever sponsored one of its own before, and we want to be the first! You go to China, and we will supply the money."

Jonathan was speechless. Tears flooded his eyes as he searched for words to thank his classmates. The same men who had taunted and mocked him three and a half years before now wanted to send him out as their representative. Jonathan now had a way to serve in China, and he could not have been happier about it.

As Jonathan's time at Knox College drew to a close, he was asked to speak in many churches about his plans. He was so enthusiastic about missionary work, however, that not every church he visited was glad they had invited him!

One Sunday the pastor in charge of home missions for the Presbyterian Church in Canada invited Jonathan to speak at his church, Zion Church in Brantford. The church members were proud of the amount of money they had raised for home missions within Canada. However, Jonathan had studied the foreign missionary giving for each church in the area and knew that Zion Church gave only seventy-eight cents per person per year to foreign missions. Jonathan was appalled. He arrived at the church ready to challenge the congregation about their giving and undaunted by the pastor's prominent position in the church hierarchy.

Jonathan's opportunity to deliver his challenge was not long in coming. The opening hymn was announced, and the choir director read the first verse aloud before the singing began:

From Greenland's icy mountains,
From India's coral strand...
Waft, waft, ye winds His story,
And you, ye waters, roll,
Till like a sea of glory
It spreads from pole to pole.

When the choir director had finished reading, the organist poised her hands, ready to peal out the first bars of the hymn. As she did so, Jonathan sprang to his feet, his hands raised to stop the singing. He bounded to the pulpit and boomed, "No! No! A congregation like this one does not have the right to sing that hymn." He waved the blue book containing the church's financial records high in the air. "You are a large and prosperous group, yet you give only seventy-eight cents apiece to foreign missions! This is not a hymn you have earned the right to sing. Let's sing Psalm 51 instead."

He gave the organist a stern look, and she nervously flipped through the pages of her music book until she found the music for Psalm 51. The congregation obediently sang along with Jonathan, who then preached from the story of the loaves and the fishes.

The story tells of how more than five thousand people followed Jesus to hear Him teach. As night approached, the disciples wanted to send the crowd away because they had nothing to feed them. Just then a young boy came forward with five loaves of bread and two fish. Jesus blessed the food, broke it into pieces, and told the disciples to distribute it to the crowd. Everyone had enough to eat, and afterwards there were twelve basketfuls of leftovers.

When Jonathan had finished retelling the story, he said, "Now, let's imagine for a moment that the disciples fed the first two rows of people. When they were done, instead of moving on to feed the back rows, they went to the front and fed the first two rows a second and then a third time. After a while, people in the first two rows were so full they turned away when food was offered to them. All the while, the people in the back rows were fainting from hunger."

Jonathan paused for a moment to let the congregation think about what he had said. "My friends," he continued, "aren't we doing the same thing when we put most of our time and money into giving the Bread of Life to those who have heard it so often while millions of people in China are starving for the gospel message?"

When Jonathan had finished his sermon, the church sat silently thinking about the simple yet powerful point he had made.

Finally, on October 25, 1887, after being engaged for a year, Jonathan Goforth and Rosalind Bell-Smith were married. The ceremony was held a week after Jonathan was ordained as a pastor. Following the wedding, the Goforths were to spend six months traveling and speaking at churches in Canada before setting sail for China. Although their wedding went as planned, their departure for China did not. In late 1887, China was in the grip of a desperate famine, and the Presbyterian Church in Canada had raised a large sum of money to help with the disaster. It needed someone to take the money to China as quickly as possible and make sure it was placed in the right hands. Jonathan was asked whether he could be ready to leave for China with the money by mid-January.

Jonathan was eager to get to China as soon as possible, and so he wasn't too worried about the earlier departure date. Rosalind, though, was disappointed. The women at Uxbridge Presbyterian Church had donated a beautiful twenty-four-stop organ for her and Jonathan to take to China. In their rush to get to Vancouver, British Columbia, from which they were to leave for China, they had no time to wait for the organ to be crated and shipped. Jonathan told Rosalind that it would have to follow them to China on a later boat.

The newlyweds hurriedly packed their belongings. Rosalind's mother had died a few months previously, and so Rosalind took with her several special items from the family home, including a self-portrait her father had painted and some of her mother's favorite china plates and cups.

The commissioning service in which Jonathan and Rosalind dedicated their lives for service in China was held on January 19, 1888, at Knox Church in Toronto. The huge church was filled to overflowing for the service, and the crowd spilled out into the street. All sorts of people were there—pastors, college professors, workers from the eastside mission, and hundreds of poor people Jonathan had visited during his four years in the city. Many people got up to speak at the commissioning, and in the end, the service had to be cut short so that the Goforths could get to Old Market Station in time to catch the Trans Canada train at midnight.

Jonathan and Rosalind walked the half mile to the train station surrounded by hundreds of their friends and coworkers. At the station, the group sang hymns until the conductor yelled, "All aboard!"

They had just enough time for one last parting prayer, and then to the sound of the crowd singing "Onward Christian Soldiers," Jonathan helped Rosalind onto the train. He quickly found their compartment and rolled down the window and peered out, trying to fix one last image of family and friends in his mind.

The engine belched smoke and steam, and the whistle wailed as the train slowly pulled away from the station. As the train rounded a corner after leaving the station, the sound of the singing finally faded and Jonathan closed the window.

"Let's pray," said Jonathan, bowing his head and reaching for Rosalind's hand. "Lord," he began, "we don't know what lies ahead of us, but we pray that whatever happens, You will make us worthy of the great trust so many people have placed in us."

Chapter 4

China at Last

Jonathan and Rosalind Goforth stood on the dock staring up at the freshly painted hull of the SS *Parthia.* They had just arrived in Vancouver, British Columbia, and had arranged to board the ship a day early because there were no hotel rooms available in the city. A huge fire had recently swept through town, destroying most of the wooden buildings.

"She looks seaworthy enough," said Jonathan, tucking his wife's arm in his. "Let's go aboard."

Jonathan led the way up the gangplank, breathing deeply as he savored the salt-laden sea air. He had been on the Great Lakes many times, but he had never before experienced the sight, sound, and smell of the ocean. Once on board, the couple were shown to their cabin. Located on the starboard side of the ship, the small cabin would be comfortable enough for the two-week voyage.

The following morning, February 4, 1888, Jonathan watched eagerly as first the stern line and then the bowline that secured the SS *Parthia* to the dock were let go and the ship slipped out into Vancouver harbor. The SS *Parthia* glided around the southern end of Vancouver Island. The sea was calm as the ship passed the city of Victoria and made its way through the Strait of Juan de Fuca, bordered to the south by the majestic Olympic Mountains. Soon afterwards the ship headed out into the Pacific Ocean.

As they hit the open sea, there was a slight swell, and Jonathan noticed that the ship pitched and rolled under his feet more than he had expected it would. The pitching and rolling soon drained the color from Rosalind's face, and Rosalind excused herself and went below to the cabin to lie down for a few minutes. As the waters of the northern Pacific became rougher, the few minutes lying on her bed feeling seasick turned into hours, and then days.

The voyage quickly turned into a nightmare for Jonathan and Rosalind. It was hard for them to believe that a ship could pitch and heave as much as the SS *Parthia* did. Even when the sea was calm, the ship rolled violently. Halfway through the voyage, Jonathan found out why. The SS *Parthia* was twenty-five years old, and for most of those years she had been a cargo passenger ship plying the waters of the North Atlantic between London and New York. The ship had been poorly designed, and after a while her reputation for pitching and rolling had become so well known that no one would book passage on her. Wanting to keep making money, the ship's owner had brought the vessel to the West Coast of North America to sail the Pacific Ocean. The ship had been repainted and renamed the SS *Parthia,* and the Goforths were passengers on her "maiden voyage" in the Pacific. Jonathan didn't think it would be too long before the ship had a reputation in the Pacific as well.

Eventually the terrible ordeal ended, and the SS *Parthia* docked in Kobe, Japan. Jonathan and Rosalind transferred to a much more stable ship for the final leg of the voyage across the Yellow Sea to Shanghai.

In 1888, Shanghai was known as the jewel of China. It was the place where East met West. It was also a bustling international port city as modern as Paris or London. As the ship moved upriver, Jonathan stood on deck and watched as the great city came into focus. Despite the bustle and varied architecture of Shanghai, Jonathan had little interest in exploring the city for its own sake. He was eager to begin the work he had spent the past four years training for.

As soon as the ship docked, Jonathan disembarked and found a boardinghouse where he and Rosalind could stay. Since there was no Canadian Presbyterian mission in Shanghai or anywhere else in China, he set off to find the headquarters of the China Inland Mission, where he arranged a meeting with other missionaries for the next day. That night as Jonathan and Rosalind dined simply on chicken and rice, Jonathan made notes on the points he needed to cover in his discussions the next day.

At the meeting the following day, missionaries from four other missions were waiting to greet the first Canadian Presbyterian missionary to China. After the formal introductions were completed, these missionaries from various denominations got down to business. Jonathan handed over the large sum of money that had been raised in Canada for famine relief, and then the other missionaries set to advising Jonathan as to which part of China the Canadian Presbyterian Church should focus on as its mission field. By midafternoon it had been decided: The Goforths and any missionaries who joined them would work in the North Honan area, a stretch of land bordered by the Yellow River, the Gobi Desert, and the East China Sea. It was suggested that before the Goforths headed there, they should go to Chefoo, four hundred fifty miles north of Shanghai on the coast. They could stay there near the China Inland Mission station while they learned the basics of the Mandarin language.

Jonathan was pleased by the outcome of the meeting, and he was eager to leave for Chefoo right away. However, one of the missionaries at the meeting persuaded him to stay one more day so that he could visit the famous opium palace of Shanghai.

The opium palace lay in the International Settlement, the part of Shanghai controlled by various European countries. The palace was a magnificent building, well lit and decorated with brilliantly colored silks. Entering it was like entering another world for Jonathan. In each room of the building were narrow beds neatly arranged in rows. On the beds lounged hundreds of Chinese people, many of them well dressed, and all of them high on opium. Some of the people seemed healthy enough to Jonathan, but others had sunken cheeks and rotting teeth. Most of them never even bothered to look up as he and Rosalind squeezed between their beds.

After they had walked through several rooms, the missionary guide led Jonathan and Rosalind out into the narrow street that bordered the palace. Both sides of the street were lined with brothels. Jonathan stood staring at it all for a long time before turning to the guide. "How can this be?" he asked, the heartbreak he felt betrayed in his voice. "The palace and these brothels—they're in the section of Shanghai controlled by foreign governments."

"Yes, I'm afraid they are," replied the missionary guide. "There is no excuse for a building like this being set aside solely to get Chinese people addicted to opium. It's all about greed. Selling opium to the Chinese makes lots of money for foreign governments, particularly the British."

Jonathan could scarcely believe what he was hearing. "Do you mean to tell me the British are supplying the opium and allowing these prostitutes to work in their own territory?"

The missionary nodded. "It's difficult for the Chinese people to understand that we missionaries mean them good when others from 'Christian' countries encourage such evil practices in their land."

"No wonder they call us foreign devils," interjected Rosalind indignantly.

"Yes. And because the Chinese can't strike back at these foreign governments, they often strike back against the missionaries serving in rural areas. I'm sure you're aware that a number of missionaries have been killed recently."

Jonathan sat in silence as a rickshaw carried him and Rosalind back to their boardinghouse. He was eager to get to Chefoo. There was so much that needed to be done in China, and Jonathan had a dark feeling deep inside that there might not be much time to do it.

A week later Jonathan and Rosalind felt like "real" missionaries. They had rented a long, narrow house with a thatched roof, and Rosalind had started unpacking their belongings and turning the house into a home. The process took her longer than it normally would have, since she was expecting a baby in August and tired easily. Meanwhile, Jonathan hired a Mandarin tutor and threw himself into language learning, helping his wife with the unpacking on his spare evenings.

One night, as Jonathan and Rosalind were finishing dinner, they heard a commotion outside.

Jonathan slipped out the door and into the street to see what was going on. He didn't have to ask. As he looked in the direction everyone was pointing, he froze in horror. The roof of their house was swathed in crackling orange flames, and clumps of fiery thatch from the roof were falling into the back rooms of the house.

"God, help us!" said Jonathan as he turned to look into the panicked eyes of his wife, who had followed him outside. "Stay here," he ordered. "I'm going inside to see what I can rescue."

Jonathan ran back into the living room where only moments before he had been enjoying dinner. He scurried into the bedroom and grabbed his study Bible and the money jar. As he dashed out, thick smoke began to fill the house.

"Here, Rosalind, hold these," he yelled, passing the Bible and money jar to his shocked wife. "I'm going back for more."

Jonathan was just about to enter the burning house again when he turned to see Rosalind running around in circles, her eyes glazed and distracted. Three Chinese men were moving closer to her. "For goodness sake, Rosalind," he yelled. "Pull yourself together. Hold on to that jar or someone will steal it."

Jonathan's comments snapped Rosalind out of her panic. She stopped running in circles and held tightly to the money jar and her husband's Bible.

Jonathan entered the house again. The smoke was chokingly thick by now, and burning thatch was falling all around. Jonathan grabbed his wife's sewing machine and his Mandarin language study notes. He could hear the crackling of the fire on the roof above him as he fled the building.

Outside, Jonathan and Rosalind stood and watched helplessly as everything they had brought with them from Canada, including their wedding presents, the portrait of Rosalind's father, her mother's china, and the delicately knitted shawl her sister had made for their first baby, went up in flames.

As the fire began to die down, Jonathan turned and looked into the tear-streaked face of his wife. "Don't worry, dear," he said, comfortingly. "They were just things."

That night Jonathan and Rosalind stayed at the China Inland Mission boarding school and returned the following morning to survey the damage in the light of day. There was nothing left of their home but a pile of smoldering ashes.

"We'll be all right," said Jonathan, as cheerful as ever. "God will supply all of our needs. And think of it, Rosalind. We were upset because that beautiful organ could not travel with us. Look what would have happened to it if we'd had it with us now. Instead, it is safe and on its way to us."

His wife looked up at him and smiled weakly. "I think it will be a long time before I learn to see the good in everything as you do, Jonathan Goforth," she replied.

A week later Jonathan and Rosalind were settled into their second home in Chefoo and were busily studying Mandarin. Many missionaries in the area kindly gave them furniture, household goods, and clothes. The Goforths also received their first monthly support check from the alumni at Knox College. Despite the fire, Jonathan was surprised by how little they could live on if they were frugal. By April, which marked the first six months of their marriage, Jonathan had been able to give away to other missions the equivalent of ten percent of an entire year's income. Jonathan was very pleased by this. Being a missionary was not nearly the financial burden he had expected. After balancing the account book, he went off to announce the good news to his wife. He proudly told Rosalind that they had already given enough money for a year's tithe and they still had six months to go. "What do you think we should do about it?" he inquired.

Rosalind looked up from her sewing with a puzzled look on her face. "Well, if we have given ten percent of our yearly income already, I don't suppose we need to give any more until October," she replied.

Jonathan sat down and stared at his wife. "Do you really think so?" he asked. "I was thinking the Lord has been so good to us that we should try to give another ten percent before the end of the year."

"Well," replied Rosalind hesitantly, "if you think that's really what we should do with the baby coming and all…"

Jonathan left the conversation hanging, but over the next couple of days, Rosalind agreed that they should continue to give money to other missionaries. By the end of the year, they had given one fifth of their income away.

Jonathan plodded on with his language studies. As the summer approached, the weather seemed to get hotter and hotter. When Jonathan complained about it to some of the other missionaries, they told him the heat of Chefoo was nothing compared to the searing summer heat of the inland provinces where the Goforths would be serving. In late summer the Goforths' first child, a healthy daughter whom they named Gertrude, was born on August 12, 1888. Jonathan and Rosalind prayed she would stay healthy, especially since there was an outbreak of cholera in Chefoo.

As the summer wound down, Jonathan Goforth's plans began to take shape. He decided that his small family should move to Pangchwang, an American Board mission station located several days' journey inland and closer to North Honan, their final destination. In Pangchwang, the Goforths continued their language studies, though Jonathan found learning the language difficult. Despite this, he was not discouraged but kept studying as hard as he could. Rosalind, on the other hand, was soon speaking fluent Mandarin.

From Pangchwang, Jonathan made several journeys into North Honan in preparation for moving his family there. Not only was he excited about what lay ahead, but also he was excited when his best friend from Knox College, Donald McGillivray, wrote to say he was coming to China to help set up the mission station in North Honan. Soon after Donald arrived, the small band of Canadian Presbyterian missionaries made plans to move from Pangchwang to Linching, a city located on the banks of the Wei River about fifty miles closer to North Honan.

Chapter 5

Sorrow and Success

"Hold it steady," Jonathan Goforth yelled as he prepared to jump onto the small wooden boat.

Two of the Chinese boatmen reached out and pulled him aboard.

"Hand me Gertrude," Jonathan said, turning back to Rosalind, who was still standing on the dock.

Rosalind passed the ten-month-old child to her husband and then climbed aboard the boat herself.

Soon the Goforth family was seated in the center of the bobbing craft, ready for the next leg of their journey, a two-day trip up the Wei River to Linching. Donald McGillivray had gone on ahead and sent back word that the building renovations were almost complete and it was time for Jonathan and Rosalind to join him there.

Even though it was still early morning as the boat began making its way upriver, the sun beat down mercilessly. The air was stifling hot, and Jonathan watched with concern as Gertrude labored for each breath she took.

"We need a way to cool her down," said Rosalind, her voice raised in motherly concern.

"Yes," replied Jonathan. "I had no idea how spoiled we were being by the coast last summer. The captain says the temperature will be over one hundred degrees for most of the trip."

Rosalind groaned and rolled up the sleeves of her blouse. "Here, help me to find our sheets. I have an idea," she said.

Jonathan opened their large wicker suitcase and rummaged around in it until he found two cotton sheets.

"I was thinking we could dip them in the water and then hang them over us," Rosalind told her husband.

Jonathan nodded and followed his wife's instructions.

Soon the three of them were sitting in the shade of the dripping wet sheets which, besides filtering out the sun, managed to lower the temperature around them a degree or two.

As the boatmen rhythmically paddled the boat, Jonathan pulled his Bible from a small leather bag. Tucked inside the Bible was a letter from Hudson Taylor, founder of China Inland Mission. Hudson Taylor had heard that the Canadian Presbyterian mission had been given the Honan region as its mission field in China, and he had written to offer Jonathan some advice. In the letter he said, "Brother, if you would enter that province, you must go forward on your knees."

Jonathan sat for a long time thinking about Hudson Taylor's advice in the letter. It was true, if he was going to achieve anything in his new mission field, it was going to come as the result of prayer. So right there Jonathan began to pray for the people who inhabited the many tiny villages and towns they passed on their way upriver to their new mission station.

When the boat finally arrived in Linching two days later, everyone was sore and stiff. True to his word, Donald McGillivray had everything under control. Renovations of the Goforths' new home were almost complete, and Jonathan and Rosalind moved in.

From the very first night in the house, Jonathan noticed a foul odor in the neighborhood. He concluded that the house next door must have a dead animal rotting in its courtyard. However, the next day Jonathan discovered he had to look no farther than his own house to find the source of the stench.

Chinese workers were busy constructing a brick wall around the house, and Donald McGillivray had instructed them to get the water for the mortar from a nearby well. Eager to save themselves some effort, the workers had found a pond closer to the house from which to draw their water. But the pond was an open sewer, and the water the workers were using to mix the mortar was the source of the foul odor. As soon as Jonathan realized what they were doing, he insisted the workers walk the extra distance to the well to get clean water. He explained that not only did the water from the pond smell bad and attract flies but also it could make them ill.

Jonathan's warning came too late, however. Many of the workers became ill with dysentery, and soon little Gertrude Goforth also came down with it. Dr. Perkins, a missionary with the American Board, helped Jonathan and Rosalind as much as she could as they battled to save their curly-haired little daughter. When Rosalind also got sick with dysentery, Jonathan became frantic with worry. He fretted that he was about to lose both his wife and his daughter.

Gertrude vacillated between life and death for six days until finally her tiny body could take no more. She died on July 24, 1889, twenty days after arriving in Linching and less than a month short of her first birthday. Rosalind, though, continued to cling to life.

In Linching, since there was nowhere to bury a foreigner, Jonathan hired a cart and, accompanied by Donald McGillivray, set out to take Gertrude's body back to Pangchwang, where she could be buried in the mission cemetery. While he was in Pangchwang, Jonathan penned a letter to friends back in Canada.

None but those who have lost a precious treasure can understand our feelings, but the loss seems to be greater because we are far away in a strange land..."All things work together for good." The Lord has a purpose in taking our loved one away. We pray that this loss will fit us more fully to tell these dying millions of Him who has gained the victory over death.

After arranging a funeral service and burying Gertrude beside the graves of two other missionary children, Jonathan Goforth and Donald McGillivray hurried back to Linching. Throughout the journey, Jonathan prayed that Rosalind would still be alive when he got back. He couldn't bear the thought of making the same trip again to bury his wife. Thankfully, on his arrival, Rosalind was showing some sign of improvement. Eventually, after a slow recovery, she was able to rejoin Jonathan in language study.

Apart from the death of his daughter, Jonathan found language study to be the most difficult thing about living in China. The situation was made even more frustrating because Donald McGillivray was so good at the language. Even though Donald had been in China a year less than Jonathan, he had already memorized all of the characters in the Chinese version of the Gospels while Jonathan was still struggling to learn the first half of them.

This lack of progress in language proved most frustrating when it came to chapel time. The two missionaries took turns reading the Bible and explaining to the local Chinese people what it meant. More often than not, though, when it was Jonathan's turn to read and speak, the people would beg him to sit down and let Donald McGillivray speak in his place. "We understand him, not you," they would say to Jonathan as they pointed to Donald. "He talks our way."

Jonathan could not blame them, yet he knew he could never go into the North Honan region unless he spoke Chinese well. He began to question whether he was capable of learning the language. He tried just as hard as Donald McGillivray at language study, but somehow he didn't seem to have a knack for the language.

One day, after he had been in Linching for several months, Jonathan grew desperate. He hated it when it was his turn to preach, knowing that even the most patient Chinese person couldn't make too much sense of what he said. As he left the house that day, he said to Rosalind, "If the Lord does not work a miracle for me with this language, I fear that I'm going to be a complete failure as a missionary!"

The walk to the chapel took about twenty minutes. As he walked, Jonathan prayed silently, asking God to help him unlock the keys to the Chinese language. Later, when he got up to speak at the chapel service, everything he had studied about the language seemed to come into focus. Jonathan listened to himself as he spoke, amazed at how well he was putting together the Chinese words. He had never been able to speak like that in Chinese. The Chinese people listening noticed, too. In fact, when Donald McGillivray got up to speak, the crowd yelled to Jonathan, "No, you keep going."

Jonathan could hardly wait to get home and tell Rosalind about the breakthrough he had experienced with the language. He still had a lot of study to do before he was completely fluent in Chinese, but after his experience at the chapel service, he had confidence that he could master the language.

In the meantime, in preparation for moving to North Honan, Jonathan had begun making trips into the area, often accompanied by one of the medical doctors who served with the American Board. On one such trip in the fall of 1889, Jonathan and Dr. McClure set off together to visit Hsunhsien, where they met the magistrate of the city, who invited them both to dinner. After talking for a while during the meal, the magistrate's voice grew very serious. "Sir," he said, turning to the doctor, "my old chief of police has gone blind. Would you be kind enough to take a look at his eyes and see if there is anything you can do for him?"

"Certainly," replied Dr. McClure. "Send for him."

The magistrate turned and barked an order to his servant. Ten minutes later an elderly man was led into the room.

"This is Mr. Chou, whom I told you about," said the magistrate.

The two missionaries greeted the blind man, and then Dr. McClure examined the man's eyes. It took only a minute or two to make a diagnosis. "Mr. Chou, you have cataracts over both of your eyes. It will not be difficult to remove them and give you your sight back," said the doctor.

"Ah!" exclaimed the old man in delight. "I am ready. When can we begin?"

"I cannot perform the operation right now," apologized Dr. McClure. "I am due back in Linching next week, and I would need to stay with you for two weeks after such an operation. I will come back in six months, and I will stay long enough to operate on you and look after you."

Jonathan watched as the smile on Mr. Chou's face turned to a scowl. "Take me away from here," Mr. Chou said to the man who had led him into the room. The two men stood and left, but Jonathan could hear Mr. Chou complaining as he walked away.

"Ha! That doctor is a fraud and a liar. He tried to impress the magistrate by telling him he could heal a blind person, but he cannot. He says he will be back in six months, but I do not believe it. He is only pretending. Foreign devil!" the old man snarled.

The two missionaries and the magistrate sat in silence for a moment. Finally the magistrate broke the silence. "I must apologize for the old man. He was the chief of police, you know, and they are not noted for their manners."

Jonathan nodded. He had experienced enough of China to know that the chief of police was often the most corrupt person in a town or village. The chief of police received no salary from the government. Instead, he was expected to extract his salary by way of bribes and other payments from the people he served. This system often led to guilty men going free while innocent men went to prison in their place.

"We will be back," Dr. McClure said firmly, "and we will stay for two weeks so that I can nurse Mr. Chou back to health."

True to their word, six months later, Jonathan and Dr. McClure returned to Hsunhsien. While the old chief of police was shocked to hear they had returned, he was nonetheless eager for the operation to restore his sight.

Dr. McClure set up a makeshift surgery unit, and Jonathan acted as his assistant. The operation was a simple but delicate procedure and was over quickly. The doctor then held up his hand. "How many fingers do you see, Mr. Chou?" he asked.

A huge smile spread across the old man's face. "Five," he said. "I can see five fingers!"

"Wonderful," replied Dr. McClure. "Now I will bandage your eyes so that they can rest and heal properly. In two weeks we will take the bandages off, and you should be able to see again."

For the next two weeks, Mr. Chou stayed with Jonathan and Dr. McClure, who included him in everything they did, from prayer meetings to preaching in the open air. At first Mr. Chou could not understand the message they preached. He could not believe that God loved everyone, even someone who had done as many wicked and corrupt things as he had. Over the two weeks he was with the missionaries, though, he began to believe what they told him. By the time his bandages were removed, Mr. Chou had become a Christian. His wife soon followed his example, and together the couple began preaching in the streets of Hsunhsien.

One day soon after his sight had been restored, Mr. Chou was preaching with Jonathan near the temple of a goddess who was supposed to be able to grant male children to men who made sacrifices to her. Since having a son was a point of great pride to Chinese people, many men came from hundreds of miles away to ask the goddess for help. On this particular day, the mayor of a neighboring town was leading a huge procession up the hill to the temple. In his arms he was carrying a paper model of a baby boy that he was going to burn as a sacrifice in the temple in hopes that the goddess would send him a real son.

When the throng was about halfway up the hill, Mr. Chou began yelling at them. "The goddess you worship has no power to give you sons! I once thought she had great powers, too. When my eyesight began to fail, I spent a lot of money bringing her sacrifices, hoping she would have pity on me, but nothing happened. Then I met the Christians, sent by the one true God. They restored my sight and also opened the eyes of my darkened soul. You know what a bad man I was, how I did not care about justice as long as I got rich, but now I am different!

God's love has come into my heart, and I want to do good things for people all the time. The Christian God is the one with power, not the goddess you are going to worship. She is just a lump of clay."

As Mr. Chou spoke, the crowd grew very quiet listening to him and watching the mayor to see what he would do. When he made no move to continue on up the hill, Jonathan took over the preaching. "I have nine brothers and one sister. My wife has nine brothers and three sisters. Our parents have nineteen sons between them, and no one where I come from has ever heard of this goddess who is supposed to grant sons. How can that be? It is the one true God who gives sons and daughters to us. It says so in His Word," shouted Jonathan, holding up his Bible. "If it is God's will that you have a son, then you will have a son. It has nothing to do with this idol or anything you might offer her."

Jonathan stopped to catch his breath, and the worshipers used the moment to urge the mayor to continue on up the hill to the temple.

"Come on," they said. "We are wasting time, and we are angering the goddess. She does not want us to stay and listen to this nonsense."

"No, no," replied the mayor. "You go on if you want to, but I am staying to hear more about this God."

Three hours later, the mayor announced he wanted to become a Christian. He threw away the paper model of the baby son and told the crowd he would wait for God to give him a son.

Jonathan could scarcely believe what had happened. In just a month he had seen his first two Christian converts, both important men in their villages, and both prepared to go and fearlessly proclaim the gospel to others. He hurried home to Linching to tell Rosalind the wonderful news.

Soon after arriving home, Jonathan received word that the mayor had become a serious student of the Bible. The mayor had memorized all four of the Gospels, and he preached whenever he had the opportunity. As a result, forty families had now denounced their idols and embraced the gospel.

December 1889 marked the birth of another child in the Goforth home. This time it was a boy, whom they named Donald, after Donald McGillivray. The boy was almost always referred to by the nickname "Wee Donald."

About this time there was another important arrival in Linching. Three couples and two single women from Canada joined the Goforths and Donald McGillivray at the mission. The night they arrived, everyone met to discuss the best way to work together. Although Jonathan was leader of the mission, he wanted everyone involved in the decision about what to do next. After talking and praying, the group took a vote on what they should do and decided they should stay on in Linching for about a year and a half while they learned the language. Once everyone was fluent in Chinese, they would be ready to fan out in pairs across Honan province.

While they were all undertaking language study, it was also decided that Jonathan, Donald McGillivray, and the other three missionary men would take turns making journeys into Honan province to scout out suitable locations to set up mission stations. Even though most foreigners and the well-to-do Chinese either were carried in sedan chairs or rode donkeys, Jonathan insisted that everyone who went "touring" with him walk. He had a simple reason for this. In Linching, Jonathan noticed that several men had wanted to join the missionaries, not because they believed in the gospel but because they wanted to live like the missionaries did back in Chefoo. Jonathan, though, wanted only Chinese helpers with him who were serious about Christianity, and so he didn't allow any extra "luxuries," like riding donkeys when they could all walk.

Instead of buying sedan chairs and donkeys, Jonathan bought a used wheelbarrow for four dollars and hired a man to push it for thirty-five cents a day. The barrow was filled with books, clothing, and preaching aids. By using a wheelbarrow to transport their things and staying in the cheapest inns, Jonathan was able to tour through new areas of the province for less than fifty cents a day. At that rate, he was sure that no Chinese person looking for a life of leisure was going to join him!

Those who traveled with Jonathan would awake at daybreak and walk at least five miles before stopping for breakfast. After breakfast, the group would set off again, inquiring along the way to see whether any Christians were in the villages they passed through. If there were Christians, they would stop and encourage and pray with them before walking on to the next village. Often they would walk for eight or ten hours a day before stopping at an inn for the night. While the other members of the party rested, Jonathan liked to take advantage of the curiosity of the other guests at the inn. As soon as he had paid for a spot to sleep on the k'ang—the raised, heated sleeping platform—he would invite a crowd to gather around and listen to Bible stories. He would talk for about half an hour, and then, after they had rested, one of the other men would take over for him. It was only then that Jonathan would take off his boots and have a hot drink.

The journeys were often dangerous because throughout China there was an increasing hatred for foreigners. Jonathan suggested that he and the other missionary men wear Chinese clothing so that they could slip in and out of villages and towns unnoticed if things became violent. This strategy worked sometimes, though not always. Once, in the summer of 1890, Jonathan and one of the missionary men entered a town where an enormous crowd had gathered to watch some kind of performance. A huge tent had been set up, and people were pushing at its sides to get in. Jonathan was always careful to stay towards the back of the crowd and keep his head down. On this occasion, however, it wasn't enough.

"Foreign devils!" yelled a woman near Jonathan. In an instant the entire crowd swung around to see who had infiltrated their midst. Jonathan grabbed his companion by the wrist and took off running. He could feel rocks hitting his back, and he heard the roar of the crowd behind him. Then he heard a strange whooshing noise, followed by the creaking and then snapping of wood. Jonathan stopped fleeing and turned just in time to see the enormous tent collapse. The foreign devils were forgotten, and the crowd surged back to pull people from the collapsed tent. Jonathan and his companion used the opportunity to get away, but the incident reminded them that there were many Chinese people who wanted all foreigners dead.

After making visits into the Honan region for eighteen months, the missionaries decided the time for their move into the area was drawing near. However, Jonathan would first have to make one more trip. By now Rosalind had given birth to another son, Paul, and she juggled her days by watching the boys, studying the language, and running the mission house.

One day, when Wee Donald was eighteen months old, he was running around the veranda of their house. Jonathan tried to catch him, but Donald thought it was a game and ran faster. He grabbed one of the posts and began swinging around it and laughing wildly. Then, suddenly, he lost his grip and went sailing through the air. Jonathan watched in horror as Donald fell to the ground, hitting his head on a flowerpot as he did so. Jonathan rushed to his son, and he was greatly relieved when Wee Donald opened his eyes and smiled at him.

"Thank God, no harm was done," he said, lifting Donald up and setting him on his knee.

Jonathan was wrong, however. While Wee Donald seemed to have no immediate problems from his fall, over the next few weeks he became very sick. Bit by bit his arms and legs stopped working, and Jonathan and Rosalind decided the best thing to do was to take him to Shanghai to see a specialist. Towards the end of July 1891, Wee Donald found it hard to hold up his head, and then to breathe. He died peacefully on July 25. Jonathan took his little body back to Pangchwang to be buried alongside his sister, Gertrude.

It was a sad journey. The Goforths had been in China for three and a half years, and in that time two of their three children had died. The only thing that gave Jonathan comfort was the missionary work awaiting him in Honan province.

Chapter 6

Changte

Just as Jonathan Goforth had expected, the first years at Chuwang, deep inside Honan province, were not easy. The Chinese people were becoming more resentful of foreigners and angry at the way they were interfering in the running of their country. Posters went up all round the country telling of the evil things the foreigners did. As was to be expected in this type of atmosphere, it wasn't long before the Goforths became the target of nasty rumors. One man told how he had seen boatloads of small, drugged Chinese children being carried into the Goforths' home. He told of how, as he peered through the window, he had supposedly seen Jonathan kill the children and cut out their eyes and hearts. He claimed that the extracted body parts were used to make the powerful medicine for curing the local people. The bodies of the children were then said to be preserved in giant jars.

Many poor Chinese people had never seen a foreigner before, and they believed what they were told. As a result, very few people were brave enough to come to Jonathan's home, and fewer still were willing to listen to the gospel message that Jonathan had brought with him to present to them. Mr. Chou, the old police chief who had been cured of blindness, had come to help at the mission. He, along with the others, lived under constant threat of death, and no innkeepers would allow the missionaries to stay the night in their inns.

Jonathan learned an important lesson during this time. A foreigner must never stand in the center of a crowd but must always have his back against a solid wall. This was because Chinese people would seldom throw rocks or bricks at a person who was looking at them; they preferred to do it while their victim was not watching. By standing with a wall behind him, Jonathan was able to keep his eye on everyone and in turn reduce the number of objects thrown at him. Even when the crowd became hostile, shouting abuse and threats, Jonathan found it was best not to make a run for it but rather to stand and stare down the crowd.

After several months of foreigners living under near siege conditions, the British minister in Peking demanded of the Chinese government that all foreigners, including missionaries, be treated fairly and with respect. After this, the rumors began to die down, and a few curious Chinese people began to listen to what Jonathan had to say.

By the time the Goforths were ready to return to Canada for their first furlough in June 1894, Jonathan had his eye on the city of Changte as the site for a new mission station. Over the previous two years he had repeatedly asked the other missionaries who made up the Canadian Presbyterian contingent in China for permission to set up the new mission in Changte. Each time the group voted on the matter, the answer was always the same: no. There were not enough missionaries to spare at the existing stations to help establish a new work.

Finally, just before leaving on furlough, Jonathan was given permission to move to Changte, along with Donald McGillivray, on one condition: He was not to ask the other mission stations in the area to provide staff for the new outpost. He would have to find his own workers. This was fine with Jonathan, who was certain that once he got to Changte things would go well. First, though, it was back to Canada for furlough with Rosalind, three-and-a-half-year-old Paul, and daughter Florence, who had been born the year before.

As they were packing for the trip, a terrible flood hit Chuwang and the surrounding area. The river rose so high that the mission house was under eight feet of water. The Goforth family waited on the roof for the flood to subside, knowing that everything they owned was being destroyed by the swirling, muddy water below them. What the water did not ruin, the black mold that followed the receding river did. The only thing Jonathan was able to dry out and save was the twenty-four-stop organ. The irony of the situation was not lost on Jonathan. Soon after they had arrived in China, everything he and Rosalind owned had been destroyed by fire. Now they were preparing to leave, and everything they had accumulated since the fire had been ruined by the flood.

The trip by boat back to Canada was much smoother and more pleasant than their voyage out, though their time in Canada was rather frustrating. Jonathan spoke at eight or ten meetings a week, and while he enjoyed visiting old friends and family and telling them about the work in China, his heart was back in Honan province, where he longed to be.

Rosalind Goforth was expecting another baby, and Jonathan waited until the child was born on September 22, 1894, before he returned to China to set up the new mission station in Changte. He arranged for Rosalind, Paul, Florence, and the new baby, Helen, to make the return trip two months later, when Helen was old enough to make the journey safely.

From the moment Jonathan arrived back in China, things went well for him. While he had been away, Donald McGillivray had purchased a perfect building site for the new mission station at Changte, just outside the city wall. Jonathan agreed to stay put and supervise the building of a house and chapel on the site while Donald traveled around outlying areas preaching.

Supervising the building was not an easy task. The Chinese made it a game to see how much they could steal from the gullible foreigners. As a result, Jonathan spent much of his time making sure the materials he bought were used for the mission buildings and not whisked away by the builder for some other project. He was constantly weighing bricks and measuring lengths of wood to make sure they had not "shrunk."

By the time Rosalind arrived from Canada with the children, the buildings were finished. The house was a simple wooden structure with a dirt floor, like most of the other houses in Changte. Word quickly spread around the city that foreign missionaries had arrived in their midst. These foreigners had come with a box that made music (the organ), three pale children with hair the color of wheat, and a woman with a man's feet (almost all Chinese women at this time had their feet bound from the time they were children and were unable to walk more than a few yards at a time).

From the day the Goforth family moved into their new home, hordes of Chinese people flocked around the place trying to catch a glimpse of the foreigners. It was too good of an opportunity to miss, and Jonathan and Rosalind took full advantage of it to present the gospel, thinking the number of visitors to their new house would soon level off. Instead, the opposite happened. More and more people became curious about the foreigners living in Changte and flocked to see them.

It was only a matter of weeks before the Goforths were exhausted. Jonathan was preaching for eight or more hours a day in the chapel while Rosalind talked to the thousands of women who came to visit. Sometimes Rosalind talked so much that her voice gave out and she would have to send a note to Jonathan asking him to come and help her. By the end of their first month in Changte, Jonathan didn't know what to do. He had agreed not to ask for workers from the other mission stations, but he and Rosalind desperately needed more workers to help them.

One morning, while it was still dark, Jonathan sat reading his Bible by the light of an oil lamp. As he read, he came across Philippians 4:19: "My God shall supply all your need according to his riches in glory." The phrase "all your need" jumped out at Jonathan. "Rosalind!" he exclaimed, running into the bedroom to wake her. "God has promised to supply all our needs, and surely we need another evangelist! Let's pray right now and ask God to bring us someone."

Rosalind fixed her sleepy eyes on her husband. "But where would he come from?" she asked. "We promised not to ask for workers from the other mission stations."

"I don't know," replied Jonathan, undimmed in his enthusiasm, "but if we pray, I know God will answer us."

The two of them slipped onto their knees and prayed.

The following morning, as Jonathan was preaching in the chapel, he noticed a beggar standing at the back of the crowd. The beggar had the gaunt, haunted face of a hungry man, his clothes were dirty and torn, and he had no shoes. Jonathan presented the gospel to the crowd, and when he was done speaking, he dismissed them. As he slipped out the side door of the chapel, the beggar followed him. In the daylight, Jonathan got a better look at the man. He let out a gasp at what he saw. "Wang Fulin? Is that you?" he asked.

"Yes, Pastor, it is I," replied the beggar.

"Then you must come home for lunch with me! Rosalind will want to talk with you, too," said Jonathan.

Over the course of lunch, Wang Fulin's story came out. The Goforths had met him two years before in Linching. Although he had read through the New Testament twice and believed it was true, Wang Fulin saw no hope for himself. He was an opium addict, and no matter how he tried, he could not free himself from the grip of the drug that was slowly sapping away his life. Jonathan had finally persuaded Wang Fulin to seek help at the mission hospital, and after a long struggle, Wang Fulin's opium addiction was broken. He became a Christian, which in turn meant he had to give up running the gambling tents that had been his livelihood. With no income, he had wandered around the countryside for the past two years, often eating the bark and leaves of trees to ward off starvation.

"But yesterday," said Wang Fulin, taking a long sip of steaming tea, "I had the strange idea I should come to Changte. Do you have anything for me to do here?"

Jonathan looked at his wife. What could he say? Yesterday they had prayed for a helper, but could Wang Fulin possibly be the answer to their prayer?

"First we will get you cleaned up and fed, my friend," said Jonathan, "and then we will talk."

By midafternoon, Wang Fulin looked quite respectable in one of Jonathan's shirts and a pair of his pants. He still had sunken cheeks, and the clothes tended to hang from his bony frame.

"Would you like to come with me to preach this afternoon?" asked Jonathan.

Wang Fulin's eyes lit up. "I could think of nothing I would like better!" he exclaimed.

When Wang Fulin got up to speak, Jonathan was amazed. Wang Fulin held the crowd spellbound as he talked about how Jesus had saved him from his opium addiction. The preaching went on for three hours, and Wang Fulin seemed more energized at the end of it than he had been at the beginning.

"That was amazing!" exclaimed Jonathan as he took Wang Fulin home for dinner. "Where did you learn to speak like that?"

"Have you forgotten?" asked Wang Fulin. "A long time ago, before I ran the gambling tents, I was one of the chief storytellers of the province. I made a very good living, and people came from miles around to hear me. But," he lowered his voice, "when I started to smoke the opium pipe, my throat became sore and I could not speak loudly anymore. That is when I took up gambling."

"I see," said Jonathan, thinking that maybe God had answered his prayer after all. "Would you like to preach again tomorrow?"

Wang Fulin's face lit up in a huge smile. "Yes, please let me," he exclaimed.

Over the next few months Wang Fulin became the best evangelist Jonathan could have hoped for. Although he was never physically strong, he preached for hours at a time.

On December 16, 1895, Jonathan wrote home:

> *During the last five weeks we have had such a number of men coming day by day that we have kept up constant preaching on an average of eight hours a day. …We [Wang Fulin and Jonathan] take turns in preaching, never leaving the guest-room without someone to preach from morning to night…. Men will sit a whole half-day at a time listening. Some seem to get so much interested that they seem to forget that they have miles to go home….*

Four months later Jonathan wrote a follow-up letter. In it he said, "Since coming to Changte five months ago…25,000 men and women have come to see us and all have heard the Gospel preached to them."

Two of the first Chinese visitors to become Christians as a result of Jonathan and Wang Fulin's preaching were a well-respected doctor and a wealthy landowner. The conversion of these men had opened the way for many others who quickly followed their lead. Within months of the setting up of the mission station at Changte, small groups of Christians were meeting all over the countryside.

By mid-1896, it became obvious to Jonathan that Rosalind needed a Bible helper, too. She was expecting another baby in August, and although she kept up a grueling schedule, there was no way she could personally talk to all the women who came to visit. The problem of finding a Chinese woman who could preach seemed even more impossible than finding Wang Fulin. Still, Jonathan and Rosalind remembered how God had answered their prayer and provided Wang Fulin. Together they asked God this time to supply a suitable woman to help with the evangelistic work.

A week later Donald McGillivray returned from one of his preaching tours around the province. Among the stories he told of his exploits was one that caught Jonathan's attention. It was about the Cheng family. Cheng Ming-san was a very poor farmer who lived with his wife, three children, and his widowed mother. Both mother and son were devote Buddhists, going on long pilgrimages and giving much of their meager food to a Buddhist hermit who lived in a cave nearby. They were both active teachers of their religion.

Cheng Ming-san had a friend, also a devout Buddhist, who had become a Christian through Donald McGillivray's preaching. This man had begged Donald to go with him to the Chengs' house to share the gospel message there as well. Donald agreed, and when he got to the tiny hovel on the side of a hill where the family lived, he had found that both Cheng Ming-san and his mother were eager to hear what he had to say. Moreover, at the urging of the friend, the two of them decided to become Christians.

"And what about Cheng Ming-san's wife?" asked Jonathan.

"Well, that's another story," replied Donald sadly. "She was furious with her husband when she found out what he had done. She ran outside screaming that he would bring down judgment on them all by rejecting Buddhist ways. Although she was impossible to calm down, her husband's and mother-in-law's faith never wavered. They told me not to worry about her, that they would pray for her until she found her way to the one true God as well."

As Jonathan listened to the story, an idea began to form. "Do you think Mrs. Cheng understood what she was doing?" he asked.

"I am sure she did," Donald replied. "As soon as I prayed with them, Mrs. Cheng gathered up all of the family's idols and took them outside. She threw them into a nearby ravine, where they were smashed to pieces at the bottom. From then on she could talk of nothing else but Jesus Christ."

Jonathan became more excited. "Do you think she might agree to come here and help Rosalind?" he asked. "She has been praying for a Bible woman to help her."

Donald nodded. "Your wife should write to Mrs. Cheng at once and invite her to come. She has been a Buddhist teacher for many years, so I am sure she would jump at the opportunity to share her new faith in Jesus with others."

Later that evening, Jonathan told Rosalind of his conversation with Donald, and Rosalind sat down after dinner and wrote to Mrs. Cheng. She did not get a letter in reply. Instead, Mrs. Cheng came in person, ready to assume her new duties.

About this time, Jonathan and Rosalind also decided they needed to build a larger house. Since they were expecting another baby, the Chinese-style mission house they were living in was just too small to hold them all comfortably. Plans for a new house were drawn up. It would be Chinese-looking on the outside, but it would be filled with all sorts of Western amenities.

Chapter 7

An Open Door

"Oh, Jonathan, it's wonderful!" exclaimed Rosalind as she walked through their new house for the first time. She was carrying one-year-old Grace in her arms while the three older children trailed along behind her. Jonathan chuckled at Florence and Helen, who were both clicking their shoes loudly on the wooden floor.

"I don't suppose they remember ever walking on anything but a dirt floor before," commented Rosalind as she watched her two daughters. "I think this house is going to take a bit of getting used to."

"It sure is," interrupted six-year-old Paul. "The windows in my room have glass in them. I can see out without having to open them like I did with the shutters in the other house." Jonathan and Rosalind smiled at each other.

It took a little while for the Goforth family to explore their new home. It looked like any other Chinese house from the outside, but inside it was a treasure trove of Western ideas and gadgets. It had bedrooms with beds in them, a cooking stove, and cupboards instead of exposed shelves.

"I just hope this house is used to spread the gospel," said Jonathan, hoisting Helen up onto his shoulders to keep her out of mischief.

"I'm sure it will be," replied Rosalind. "Think of the number of people who came to visit us in the old house before we had this to show them. You know how curious the Chinese are."

Jonathan's hope was fulfilled even more than he could have imagined! News quickly spread that the Goforths had a new house filled with all manner of strange and wonderful things, which amazingly, they were willing to show to anyone who asked. It wasn't long before a crowd of men started to form outside the house at daybreak and did not disperse until long after dark. Jonathan soon developed a system that allowed the men to all see the house as well as have the gospel presented to them.

After breakfast Jonathan would stand on the veranda of the house and yell to the crowd. "Men, I have something to tell you. Stand still and listen, and then I will show you through my house."

The men would quickly settle down and listen as Jonathan preached a short sermon. When he was done he would divide the men into groups of twenty and escort them through the house.

Just as the Goforth children had done when they first saw the house, the Chinese men would stomp their feet on the wooden floor. They marveled at the chimney on the stove that let the smoke go up through the roof of the house. It was something they had never seen before. The smoke from the stoves in their houses became trapped inside. The men also opened every drawer, pulled the pillows out of the pillowcases, and turned over the mattresses to see under them. The children's toys, Grace's baby carriage, and a large tricycle made the men shake their heads in wonder.

One day, just as Jonathan was about to show a group of men down the stairs to the cellar, a group of twenty women stampeded past him, shrieking and screaming at the top of their lungs. Following behind them was Rosalind.

"What is it?" asked Jonathan.

"You wouldn't believe it," replied his wife. "The women saw a couple of china dolls in the children's room, and someone said they were tiny corpses. Next thing I knew this was happening."

Jonathan was too busy herding the men through the house to help Rosalind, who had finally caught up to the women and was trying to explain to them what they had seen. He prayed silently that she would succeed. The last thing they needed was another rumor like the one that had surfaced the year before. At that time, several local people had seen Jonathan and Rosalind drinking sweetened red vinegar with their meal and had raced around the city telling everyone that the missionaries drank the blood of children with their lunch. It had taken several weeks for the commotion this rumor had caused to die down.

When one tour was over, Jonathan would lead another one, and another one after that, until night fell. This would go on for six days a week as a seemingly never-ending tide of Chinese people came to check out the house. Of course, the tours provided lots of opportunities to present the gospel. For most of the people it was the first time they had ever heard of a loving God who cared about them and their daily lives.

While the thousands of people touring the house each week offered wonderful opportunities for Jonathan to share the gospel, they in turn had lots of opportunities to collect "souvenirs." There was no way the Goforths could watch over every person they invited in to view their house. Anything that wasn't nailed down or wasn't very large disappeared up the wide sleeves of the Chinese visitors' clothing. Cutlery, pictures, and hair combs were particular favorites for people to take. And no matter where Rosalind hid her sewing scissors, she could not keep a pair in the house. On one tour, someone took not only her scissors but also her pins, pincushion, and several half-sewn dresses she was making for the girls. As well, all of baby Ruth's bonnets and booties disappeared, and Rosalind gave up knitting new ones.

It was not easy living like this, especially for the children, but Jonathan knew it was worth the sacrifice the moment he traveled out into the surrounding countryside. Wherever he stopped, someone would come up to him and say, "It is you! I have been an honored guest in your house. You must come now and see my house." As a result, Jonathan once again had the opportunity to present the gospel to them, this time in their home.

Amid all the success Jonathan was having in his evangelistic endeavors, he also had the ongoing tragedies of missionary life to deal with. Two-year-old Grace became sick with malaria, and Jonathan and Rosalind became very worried for their daughter, especially when they noticed her stomach was beginning to swell, a sure sign of an infected spleen. Everyone at the mission station did all they could to help her, but on October 3, 1899, Grace Goforth died in her father's arms. For the third time, Jonathan and Rosalind buried one of their children in Chinese soil. This time, though, their child's body was buried under a beautiful tree in a corner of their backyard.

Soon after Grace's death, Paul, the oldest son, became ill, and it seemed likely that he too would die. Then Jonathan noticed that his own skin was turning yellow. This could mean only one thing—Jonathan had contracted hepatitis, an often deadly disease. All this occurred while Rosalind herself was in the final stages of a very difficult pregnancy—so difficult, in fact, that Jonathan wondered whether she and the child would make it through.

While it was a harrowing year for the family, thankfully Paul and Jonathan began to recover, and Rosalind safely delivered the baby on November 25, 1899. This time it was another boy, whom they named Wallace.

While all this was going on, one day in October 1899 they had the most guests ever traipse through their house. Two big events were going on in Changte at the same time. The first was the day of the semiannual fair where the city god was taken in a huge procession to a temple not far from the mission station. The second event was the administering of a government-run test. Thousands of students flooded into town to take the test. As a result, a large crowd of people began to assemble outside the Goforths' gate before dawn. By ten o'clock, five hundred men were yelling outside. Jonathan divided them into groups of one hundred fifty and first shared with them the gospel before guiding them through the house. He noticed with dismay that each time he passed through the kitchen, something else was missing, "souvenired" by the throng.

Normally when Jonathan showed a group the living room he would have Rosalind come in and play a hymn on the organ, since the Chinese were fascinated by this instrument. This day, however, everyone, including Donald McGillivray, Wang Fulin, and Mrs. Cheng, were so busy that Rosalind could not be spared, not even for the two minutes it usually took to play a hymn. Not wanting to disappoint the crowd, Jonathan sat down at the organ himself. He had no idea how to play a note on it. Still, he pulled out all the stops, pumped the pedals with his feet, and thumped his hands down on the keyboard. A dreadful booming noise erupted from the organ.

A cheer went up from the group, and Jonathan nearly fell off the organ stool when he overheard one of the men giggle with glee and say, "See, he plays better than his wife!"

At the end of the day, Jonathan was too exhausted to eat, so he drank several cups of warm milk. When the numbers were finally tallied for the day, it was easy to see why everyone at the mission was tired and a little hoarse. Eighteen hundred men and five hundred women had visited the house that day.

While this was the most people ever to tour the house in a single day, there were many days when they were nearly as busy. One particular group who came to visit often frustrated Jonathan. They were the students who had come to Changte to take the government exam. The exam would qualify them for jobs in public offices, and those whose marks were high enough might even go on to become mandarins with authority to rule over a specified area. Having enough education to take the test meant the students were usually from privileged homes, which in turn meant they were often arrogant and rude, especially towards foreigners. The students would come in groups to see the Goforths' home. However, when Jonathan tried to preach to them, they would talk loudly among themselves and tell jokes. Eventually Jonathan decided enough was enough and came up with a plan to deal with the situation. For his plan to work, he sent to Shanghai for some specific items. When the package arrived, Jonathan unpacked a large globe along with several maps and astronomical charts. Now he was ready. He waited for the next government exam to begin.

When the first group of loud, mocking students arrived, Jonathan signaled for Wang Fulin to take over preaching to the other guests while he gathered up the students and invited them back to his study. Jonathan welcomed the students and watched quietly as they were drawn to the globe he had deliberately placed on the center of his desk.

"What's that big ball?" asked one of the students.

Jonathan pretended to be surprised that anyone had noticed it. "Oh," he replied casually. "That's a small model of what the earth looks like."

"No! It can't be!" exclaimed a second student. "We all know the earth is as flat as a piece of paper."

"Yes," agreed another. "If it were a ball we would all be standing on a curve, not a flat surface."

"Not so fast," replied Jonathan. "Let me show you how we know the earth is a ball and how it turns and moves around the sun."

"Ha," interrupted another student. "I have never heard anything so ridiculous. Why, if the earth turned, we would fall off at the bottom!"

Everyone laughed loudly, and Jonathan waited patiently for them to calm down. Once they were quiet, he set about explaining to them gravity and the way the planets revolve around the sun.

As the students began to understand what Jonathan was talking about, their jeering stopped and they concentrated closely on what he had to say. It was the first time they had encountered "Western" science and its explanations of how and why the earth and the solar system work the way they do. The students were soon clamoring to know more.

After an hour or so of discussing science and answering the students' questions, Jonathan turned the conversation to God. He explained how God was not represented by an endless array of gold-covered Buddhas and other idols but rather could be known through studying the Bible and being open to its message.

Many students were fascinated by what Jonathan told them, and they came back day after day to visit him in his study. It wasn't long before a number of them had decided to become Christians. After their conversions, these students went back to their villages and towns to spread the gospel. As a result of the efforts of Jonathan and all of those at the mission station, Christian groups began to spring up all over the Changte area, until by 1900 there were over fifty groups of Christians meeting together regularly.

Not everyone was happy that Western science or religion, or any other kind of thinking, was gaining a foothold in the ancient land of China. The country was in political turmoil, and as a new century approached, China's future looked bleak.

Jonathan had great sympathy for the Chinese people's predicament. He knew that many countries, including Great Britain, the United States, Germany, France, Italy, Russia, and Japan all had their own selfish plans for China. They had met together and arranged to "carve up" China into what they called "spheres of influence." What this basically meant was that they had agreed together that each nation would take control over the trade from a certain area of China, making enormous profits for themselves and sharing little of them with the local Chinese people.

A secret society called the League of Righteous and Harmonious Fists, or Boxers, as they came to be known, sprang up to help protect China from this foreign intrusion. Its methods, however, were harsh and brutal. The members roamed eastern China, killing missionaries and traders and burning down foreign-owned buildings.

By March 1900, conditions had become very tense in the countryside. It became dangerous to travel because of the bands of thieves who waited outside the city walls. One by one, the services that connected Changte to the outside world were cut off. By June there were no more mail deliveries, and food was getting scarce. To make matters worse, there was a terrible drought in the area. Each night the wail of people pleading with their gods for rain at the various temples and shrines around Changte filled the air.

In the midst of all of this uproar, another tragedy struck the Goforths. Their seven-year-old daughter, golden-haired Florence, became ill with meningitis. Jonathan and Rosalind watched helplessly as once again another of their children died. They buried Florence beside her sister Grace. The family hardly had time to mourn, though. A few days after Florence's death on June 19, 1900, a messenger from the American consul in Chefoo slipped quietly into the mission compound under the cover of darkness. He had risked his life to bring the missionaries a letter.

The letter was brief and to the point. "Flee south. Northern route cut off by Boxers," it read. Jonathan read the note and then checked the date at the top of the page. It was dated June 2. His heart dropped. The letter had been written almost three weeks before. There was no way of knowing whether the southern route was still open or whether they should escape in another direction. Jonathan sank to his knees and prayed. The lives of his wife and children rested on what he decided they should do next.

Chapter 8

Headed West

"Mrs. Cheng told me an official courier came through Changte today on his way to Kaifengfu to deliver a message to the governor of Honan. Did you hear anything about it?" Rosalind Goforth whispered to her husband.

Jonathan looked up from the books he was packing into a box. "No," he replied, also keeping his voice low so as not to wake the children, who were sleeping in the next room. "Did she say anything else about it?"

"I'm afraid so," responded his wife. "She said he had a burnt feather in his cap and that he wore the emblem of the empress dowager."

"A burnt feather?" repeated Jonathan, the color draining from his face. It could mean only one thing: The courier was carrying a message of life or death importance. And given the rebellion in the countryside, it was most likely bad news, at least for foreigners. Jonathan suspected it could well be an order for the governor to round up all the foreigners left in his province and kill them.

"God promises in the Bible that He will lead us as a shepherd leads his sheep. That's our only hope, Rosalind," Jonathan finally said after thinking for a few moments about the courier with the burnt feather. "Let's pray we do the right thing."

Jonathan got little sleep that night. Most of the bedding had already been bundled up and loaded onto the convoy of ten hired ox-drawn carts that waited outside in the compound courtyard. As he tossed and turned, part of him wanted to stay with the other Christians at Changte, but it was too dangerous to do so, and they would not hear of it. "Go," they said. "You have done your part in bringing us the Good News. We are able to stand whatever comes, but you must take your family and go while it is still possible. We may be allowed to live, but you will surely be killed."

After receiving the warning from the American consul in Chefoo to flee, Jonathan had decided to bundle his family up and head for Fancheng in southern Honan province. There he hoped to hire a houseboat to take his family and the other missionaries at the Changte compound on the ten days' journey downriver to Hankow on the coast. Originally he had planned to take the more direct route south to Fancheng, but as he had thought about it, a strong feeling came over him that they should head in a westward direction first before looping around to get to their destination. It would be a much longer journey of two weeks by cart, but Jonathan could find no peace about taking the shorter route.

Finally Jonathan heard the clock strike 4 A.M. It was time to begin the long and dangerous journey. An hour and a half later, the Goforth family, along with nine other missionaries from the compound, among them Dr. Leslie, John Griffith, and the McKenzies and their son Douglas, were ready to go. Mrs. Cheng and Wang Fulin also insisted on accompanying them. Scores of Chinese Christians stood silently in the darkness waiting to say good-bye to the missionaries. After tying a few last items onto a wagon, Jonathan waved the convoy forward out the gate. Sitting on the lead wagon beside Wang Fulin was Rosalind, who cradled their newest baby, six-month-old Wallace, in her arms. Three-year-old Ruth sat beside her, sobbing loudly, while Helen rode on the fourth cart. She sat straight-backed, looking anxiously towards the gate and the dangers that lay beyond. Paul, on the other hand, scurried around, running between the carts, trying to help with last-minute preparations before climbing onto the cart beside his father.

Jonathan allowed himself one last look around the compound, studying the courtyard where he had preached to many thousands of Chinese people. He looked towards the study, where he had helped students unlock the wonders of the earth and the solar system, and towards the kitchen, where he and Rosalind had spent so many happy hours studying and praying together. Lastly, he diverted his eyes to the tree under which his two daughters were buried. He wondered whether he would ever be back in Changte, and if he did come back, would there be a single Chinese Christian left alive to greet him? Tears welled in his eyes as he thought about the trials that surely lay ahead for all of them, both those staying in Changte and those leaving.

A yell brought Jonathan back to the present. "God guide you every step and keep you safe, Pastor!" called out Mr. Ho, one of the church workers.

Jonathan cracked the reins. As the oxcart lunged forward, he gave one last wave to the crowd gathered to bid them farewell.

For six days they struggled slowly westward. There were many times when mobs challenged their right to be on the road, and the cry of "Foreigners! Kill the foreigners!" would go up from the crowds that gathered alongside the roads leading in and out of the villages. On the seventh day, Jonathan was very relieved when they met up with a group of foreign engineers who were also fleeing the uprising. The engineers had large wagons and armed guards to escort them to Fancheng, where they also planned to hire boats to take them to Hankow, and then go on to Shanghai.

By the time the joint party arrived at the village of Hsintien, the missionaries were exhausted. The lack of water and the burning hot sun had combined to sap their energy and, as Jonathan noted, the oxen's energy as well. It was obvious they needed to rest for a few days before traveling on. The engineers were in much better shape, since they had not come as far and were traveling in more comfortable wagons. To Jonathan's dismay, they announced they wanted to press on ahead as quickly as possible. However, they told Jonathan they were loath to leave the missionaries alone and insisted on leaving behind an armed guard on horseback for their protection.

In Hsintien, hundreds of eyes must have seen the party of engineers and all but one of their armed escorts leave early in the morning, because within minutes an angry mob had gathered outside the inn. Jonathan held Ruth close to him as he and the other missionaries listened as the crowd began to throw rocks against the doors and windows. Finally Mr. Griffith spoke. "I don't think we should stay here. I know it's not safe to go outside, but I don't see what choice we have."

"You don't expect us to go out there and harness the oxen do you?" asked the owner of one of the hired carts.

"I won't go!" exclaimed a second man. "That cart is all I own."

Jonathan sighed deeply. Since the carts and the oxen were hired, without cooperation from their owners there was no way out for the missionaries. "What if we sign a statement saying we will pay for any damages to your cart and for any oxen that might be injured or killed?" he asked one of the owners.

Even with this offer, none of the cart owners were eager to continue the journey. Eventually, after an agreement was written up and signed, they begrudgingly began to harness the oxen, which had spent the night in the stable next door.

When the cart owners had left, Jonathan took a copy of *Clarke's Scripture Promises* from his front pocket and began to read from the small book. All of the missionaries listened as he read promise after promise about how God would go with them and protect them. Jonathan was sure that everyone, even three-year-old Ruth, understood some of the risks that lay ahead on their perilous journey. It was still a long way to Fancheng, and they didn't have a single friend they could count on along the way. After Jonathan finished reading, the group prayed together, and a wonderful peace came over them all. No matter what happened, they understood they were in God's hands.

Finally the oxcarts were ready to go, and Jonathan took a deep breath. It was time to open the door and climb onto the carts. Calmly Jonathan drew back the wrought-iron bar that secured the door and stepped outside. The crowd parted for him. Mrs. Cheng followed, holding Ruth; then came the rest of the group. All went well as they climbed onto the carts. Although hundreds of people were gathered around, many of them with rocks in their hands, no one moved to stop the missionaries from leaving. There was an eerie silence as the carts rumbled over the cobblestone streets and through the town gate.

It was then that Jonathan saw them—all four hundred of them. Armed men with bags of stones and daggers gleaming from their belts were lying in wait for the missionaries around the first bend in the road. Jonathan felt his heart go cold and his arm tighten around Paul, who was sitting beside him. Before he could do anything more, a hail of stones began landing on the group, followed by something much worse: bullets. Several of the oxen were shot, and they collapsed. One fell against a rock, and Jonathan heard a sickening crunch as its back broke. Another ox, wild with panic, ran headlong into the cart in front, becoming tangled in its load.

Jonathan knew he had to act quickly before everyone was killed. He jumped down and began waving his arms furiously. "Take all of our things, but don't kill us!" he yelled in Chinese.

His words, though, seemed to enrage his enemies, who all turned their anger on him, pelting him with stones. One hit him on the side of the head. Jonathan felt warm blood oozing down his face and onto his clothes, but he kept yelling.

The mob rushed forward, energized by the sight of blood. Jonathan felt the dull thud of a heavy sword against his neck, quickly followed by a blow to the back of his head. Instinctively he raised his left arm to protect his face. As he did so, one of the mob ringleaders let out a yell of rage as over and over again the man sank his sword into Jonathan's forearm. Jonathan reached back with his other arm to steady himself against the cart, frantically looking around for his wife and children as he tried to fend off the blows. They were still on the cart. Ruth was screaming, and Rosalind held a pillow over baby Wallace to protect him from the hail of rocks that rained down on them. Just as he was about to yell to them, Jonathan felt a massive thud against the back of his skull. His knees gave way, and he fell to the ground into a puddle of his own blood. The last thing he saw before his eyes closed was the hooves of a horse galloping towards him at full speed. Then his vision went blurry and everything fell silent.

Jonathan was unconscious for only a few moments. When he came to, he saw that the horse had thrown its rider and was rearing up right in front of him. One attacker was beside him, but the others were prevented from getting any closer to him by the uncontrollable horse. As Jonathan staggered to his feet, the attacker raised his sword to deliver another powerful blow. Amazingly, he didn't. Instead he put his face close to Jonathan's and whispered urgently to him, "Get your family away from the carts."

Immediately Jonathan's mind was clear again. He wiped the blood from his face and looked around. The crowd that had been content to stand by and watch the mob kill the foreigners was now surging towards the carts, obviously intent on looting them. Shouts of rage went up from the attackers as they realized these people were going to "rob" them of "their loot."

For the next few minutes, complete chaos reigned. Men hacked at each other with swords and knives, and the women tugged at the missionaries' belongings, overturning several of the carts in the process.

Jonathan sensed that this bedlam gave him the opportunity he needed, and he staggered towards his family. "Get down from the cart," he yelled to Rosalind. "We must get away now."

Rosalind took one look at her blood-drenched husband and gasped before jumping off the cart, Wallace still in her arms protected by the pillow. The older children scrambled down off their carts, too, and Rosalind pushed through the fighting.

"Ruthie," Jonathan heard his wife cry. "Mrs. Cheng was carrying Ruth, and I can't see them."

"Come on, Rosalind," urged Jonathan. "We can't go back now. Ruth will be safe with Mrs. Cheng. We must get out of here."

Rosalind turned and trudged onward, Helen mute with fear, dragging on her mother's skirt. As they tried to escape, several men from the mob followed them, throwing rocks and jeering. By now Jonathan was barely able to concentrate on putting one foot in front of the other. His head spun, and he wanted to let go of his wife and sink to the ground.

Just then Rosalind spun around, her eyes as wild as those of a cornered mother bear trying to protect her cubs. She thrust baby Wallace into Jonathan's arms and faced their attackers. "Go ahead and kill me if you want to," she yelled above the din, "but spare the children. They haven't done anything wrong."

Much to Jonathan's amazement, the attackers stopped hurling rocks and listened to Rosalind. They looked startled to hear a "foreign devil" speaking to them in their language. As the men began arguing among themselves, Jonathan, Wallace still in his arms, sank to his knees. His head throbbed, and blood gushed from the gashes in his forearm and on the back of his head.

After what seemed the longest minute of Jonathan's life, one of the rock throwers called out, "We have killed her husband. Let her go." A roar went up from the others as they raced back to claim their share of the missionaries' goods.

"Get up," Jonathan heard his wife urging. "We're going to walk to that village over there. Perhaps they will show us mercy."

Jonathan struggled to his feet, leaning heavily on Rosalind's shoulder. One step after another Jonathan willed himself to walk towards the next village. He was barely aware of the mob that surged through its gates, rocks in hand. His last ounce of energy drained from him, and he sank to the ground once again. This time there was no reserve of strength to summon. He lay on the ground semiconscious and felt Rosalind's hand in his. His last memory was of looking up and seeing his wife kneeling over him, her tears mingling with his blood. Around him he could hear Paul and Helen sobbing loudly.

When Jonathan regained consciousness, he was lying on a pile of hay in a small brick room with only one tiny window. A flood of relief raced through him when he heard Rosalind's voice.

"I'm so glad you are all right," she said.

"What happened?" he asked, his voice raspy and weak. He felt Rosalind's hand press gently on his chest.

"Don't try to sit up," she said. "A man packed your wound with gray powder. It stopped the bleeding, but I haven't bandaged it yet."

Jonathan looked up at his wife. Her face was so swollen and bloodied he could barely recognize her. "Oh, Rosalind, are you all right?" he asked. "And what about the children? Is Ruth with us?"

"Not yet," replied Rosalind. "But I am trusting God is watching over her."

"How did we all get here?" asked Jonathan.

"It was remarkable," exclaimed his wife. "Just as you collapsed, the people from the next village came out to see what all the commotion was. The women took pity on us and persuaded the men to carry us inside the walls where we would be safer. We are in a mud hut. They locked us in for our own safety, and they have been handing hot water in through the window. They have even sent us food—stale bread and millet gruel, though no one feels like eating yet."

Throughout that day and long after the sun had set, Jonathan and his wife nursed each other and tried to comfort their children. They prayed that the other missionaries had also been able to escape and that Ruth and Mrs. Cheng were safe. They also prayed that they would somehow find a way out of their predicament.

It was the next day before they heard the door of the mud hut open. Standing silhouetted against the bright light of the sun was Mr. McKenzie. When he saw that Jonathan was still alive, he rushed to his side and began weeping. It took a full minute before he composed himself enough to talk. "Praise God, you're alive!" he said many times over.

Jonathan propped himself up on his elbows, ignoring the searing pain that shot down his neck. "Is everyone all right?" he asked anxiously. "Have you heard word of Ruth?"

Mr. McKenzie smiled down at him. "Wee Ruthie is fine," he assured them in his Scottish brogue, "though only through the bravery of Mrs. Cheng. When the mob tried to get at the child, Mrs. Cheng made her lie on the ground and then spread her body over Ruth, shielding her from the blows and rocks."

"Thank goodness for that faithful woman!" exclaimed Rosalind, tears streaming down her swollen face.

"And what of the others?" asked Jonathan.

"They are all alive, though Dr. Leslie has serious wounds. They are all waiting in a cart outside the gate. I was sent to find you so we could travel on."

Jonathan nodded. "Yes," he replied, "it's time to go on."

"But Jonathan..." Rosalind's voice trailed off as he sat up.

Mr. McKenzie helped Jonathan struggle to his feet. Jonathan leaned against the wall waiting for the dizziness to pass. Rosalind gathered the children, and then Mr. McKenzie opened the door.

Jonathan staggered forward, his head throbbing. Standing up had also opened up several of his wounds, which began to ooze blood again. He felt Rosalind's arm steadying him under his shoulder, but he gently pushed it away. "Take care of the children," he said, his voice barely audible. "Only pray the Lord will give me strength to go on as long as He has work for me to do."

Outside the mud hut a crowd of people had gathered, not the loud, jeering mob of the day before but a quiet, subdued group. Some of the women held out filthy pieces of clothing as the missionaries walked past. "Here, lady" said one woman. "We know this is not much, but it is all we have. Take these things. Your children will be cold at night, and you have nothing to cover them with."

One old man took off his shoes and ran up to Rosalind. "For you," he said, pointing to her bare feet. "To stop the stones from hurting you."

Jonathan struggled to understand why these people were being so kind to foreigners. Mr. McKenzie must have been thinking the same thing, because he asked, "Why? Why are you being so kind to us?"

"We are a Muslim village," said the old man who had given Rosalind the shoes. "How could we face our God if we joined in destroying you?"

As Jonathan staggered along the road that led out of the village, he hoped the citizens of the towns that lay ahead would show the same compassion, though deep in his heart he was sure that more danger and trials lay before them.

Chapter 9

Ku-Mu-shih

Outside the village the others were waiting on several carts that had been stripped bare of the missionaries' belongings. On one cart sat Ruth and Mrs. Cheng. And while they all had a joyful reunion, they knew many dangers still lay ahead.

Jonathan lay in the bottom of a cart beside Dr. Leslie, who was groaning with pain. "They took everything," he whispered hoarsely to Jonathan, "including my doctor's bag and my bottle of antiseptic. We have to get more from somewhere, or our wounds will become poisoned and gangrene will set in."

Jonathan lay back, too exhausted to reply.

As the oxcarts moved slowly away, the residents of the village yelled after them. "Good-bye. May God take you safely to your destination."

The road wound through a few millet fields and onto the next town, Nanyangfu. As soon as they were within a mile of the gate to this town, another huge crowd surged out to meet them. All of China seemed to be in an uproar, and the people were anxious to blame foreigners for all of their troubles. "Kill! Kill! Kill the foreign dogs!" came the cry from the crowd.

By the time the missionaries reached the town gate, the crowd had become very agitated, hurling bricks and rocks at them.

"Quickly, we must find refuge in an inn," said Mr. McKenzie. "This crowd wants blood."

He guided the oxen to the left, into the courtyard of the nearest inn. Over a thousand people surged in behind them, making it impossible to shut the gates. Without speaking, the missionaries quickly helped one another inside and bolted the door.

"Come out and show your faces, you dogs!" chanted the mass of people outside the door. The yelling kept up for over an hour, until Jonathan decided that if they did not go out, it would be only a matter of time before the crowd came in to get them.

"If we open the door, perhaps it will give one of the cart owners a chance to leave by the back way with a message for the town official pleading for him to give us safe passage through his town," said Dr. Leslie.

Everyone agreed this was a good plan, and so one of the cart owners was chosen to slip out the back door while the missionaries unbolted the front door and confronted the crowd. One by one the missionaries stepped outside and inched along the veranda with their backs to the wall. A fresh volley of insults rose from the crowd, but no one moved to attack. Jonathan and his family, along with the others, stood shoulder to shoulder facing the crowd until nightfall. It was a strange experience. It seemed that everyone wanted them dead, but no one wanted to take the first step towards killing them. Once darkness had fallen, the crowd drifted away, and the missionaries were able to go back inside. Jonathan flopped down on the k'ang; standing for such a long time had tested his physical endurance to the limit.

About an hour later, the cart owner knocked quietly on the back door and was let inside. As he sat down on the floor, every eye was fixed on him.

"Well, what happened? Will the official help us?" asked Mrs. McKenzie.

The messenger looked discouraged. "The news is not good," he replied, shaking his head. "I was not allowed to see the official myself, though the guards did take your message to him. While I was standing in the courtyard waiting for a reply, I heard two soldiers discussing the situation."

The cart owner glanced nervously at the children. Jonathan wished he could tell them to go and play while the adults talked, but they were all stuck in a single room together, and so they would just have to hear whatever came next.

"I overheard one soldier telling another that when the official read the message he immediately ordered a group of soldiers to march to a spot on the road leading west." The cart owner's voice dropped to a whisper. "Early in the morning when we pass by there, they are ordered to kill us all and make it look like a band of robbers did it."

"But how do they know we will go that way and what time we will resume our journey?" asked Rosalind.

"Ha!" said the cart owner. "The official is a clever man. He is sending some soldiers to 'protect' us. That way they will guide us right to the ambush."

There was stunned silence as everyone tried to understand the situation they now found themselves in. There was no getting around it. They would never be allowed to leave the city unless they did so under the protection of the official's soldiers, but in accepting his protection they would be guided to their deaths.

No one seemed sure of what to do, except the cart owner. "I am leaving now," he said. "I don't care what happens to my cart. You foreigners will all be dead before the morning, and I do not want to die with you. When I get back to Changte, I will tell your friends of your fate." With that he said a quick good-bye and was gone.

"What other choices do we have?" asked Dr. Leslie.

"None," replied Jonathan. "We must go on and trust ourselves to God's care."

No one was surprised when in the early hours of the morning a band of soldiers arrived at the inn. "We have come to guide you safely out of our city," one of them announced. "Quickly, we must go while it is still dark. Hitch the carts!"

Jonathan and Dr. Leslie were helped aboard the first cart, and the owner was urged to go as fast as possible by the soldiers, who appeared eager to finish their task.

The carts clattered along the ancient road and through the town gate. It was then that Mrs. McKenzie came running up to the front cart. "Mr. Griffith, is he with you?" she asked breathlessly.

Jonathan sat up and looked around. He heard Rosalind reply, "No, I thought he was in the cart with you and your husband and Paul."

Jonathan could hear the panic rising in Mrs. McKenzie's voice. "Paul? I haven't seen Paul since we were in the inn."

"Oh no!" exclaimed Rosalind. "You mean neither of them is with us?"

"I want to go back," wailed Ruth, who sat beside her mother. "I don't like the dark."

"Hush now," replied Rosalind. "We have to find Paul and Mr. Griffith."

The carts were soon stopped, and the Chinese members of the group offered to look for the missing pair while the foreigners stayed under the protection of the guards. Jonathan lay in the bottom of the cart praying for his nine-year-old son. He hoped Paul was still alive and that he was with Mr. Griffith, but none of them had any way of knowing.

As darkness began giving way to dawn, there was still no word of the whereabouts of the two missing foreigners. Eventually, the unsaid question on everyone's mind had to be asked aloud. Should they go on without the two missing members of their party? It was an agonizing decision for a parent to make, to leave a boy somewhere in a hostile city so as to try to get the others to safety. But no matter how difficult, a decision had to be made.

"We must go on," Jonathan finally whispered to Rosalind, being careful not to wake the soldiers who had crawled into the cart and were asleep alongside him. "Tell the owner of the last cart to stay behind. That's all we can do. We have to keep going."

With heavy hearts the missionaries moved on. As they did so, all the soldiers remained asleep in the carts, leaving the cart owners with little idea of which direction to take. As the sun came up, they came to a fork in the road. By this time, the cart owners themselves were nodding off to sleep, and the oxen were left to take whichever path they pleased. The first pair turned right, and the second cart followed.

About an hour later, when the sun began to warm them all, one of the soldiers woke up. "Where are we?" he demanded, rubbing his eyes.

"We don't know," replied one of the cart owners honestly, "but we have been traveling a while now."

The soldier studied the landscape and then let out a yell of protest. "It's the wrong way!"

Within seconds he had kicked the other soldiers awake, and they were all arguing over whose fault it was that they had fallen asleep.

"They went the wrong way," groaned the leader of the group, his face drained of color.

"We cannot go back!" gasped another soldier. "We have disobeyed orders."

"What will happen to us now?" whispered a third man, his eyes wide with terror.

Jonathan lay in the cart smiling to himself. Obviously, from the way they were blaming one another, the oxen had not taken the path on which the ambush had been set up.

After several more minutes of arguing, along with some punches and kicks at one another, the soldiers climbed from the carts and began walking back to town. Once they were gone, the group had only the lone rider left by the party of engineers to protect them. As the morning wore on, the carts were stopped about a dozen times by angry mobs who wanted to rob the foreigners. However, since everything had already been stolen, the travelers were allowed to continue on unharmed.

About midday a gang of bandits leapt out from behind a craggy outcrop of rocks. They swarmed around the carts, and one of them poked a long spear at the chest of one of the cart owners.

By now Jonathan was too weak to sit up, but several of the bandits jumped up onto the cart and peered down at him. "Up here," one of the men yelled to their leader.

Another man quickly jumped up onto the cart. He had long matted hair and a wild look in his eyes. Jonathan spoke calmly to him, and the man, who appeared to be the leader, stopped his cursing and threats.

Rosalind took advantage of the moment's silence. "Look," she said quietly, following her husband's example. "We have come a long way. The men are wounded, and the children are very frightened." She then grabbed some of the filthy rags the Muslim villagers had given her and continued talking. "Yet wc have met kindness along the way, and we are grateful for that. In one village the people fed us and gave us these clothes to keep the children warm at night."

Whether it was her words or the tone of her voice, Rosalind was not sure, but when the head bandit looked around at the group of wounded and bedraggled missionaries, tears formed in the corners of his eyes. He turned around to face his men. "These people have suffered enough," he yelled. "We will not bother them anymore." Then he turned to Rosalind. "This is a very dangerous road," he said with the seriousness of a good friend. "In fact, this road is so dangerous you should not go on alone. I will go with you to protect you." With that he clambered up onto the front cart and plunked himself down between Rosalind and the cart owner.

All day the bandit sat with them, fending off those who reached up to grab at the missionaries and yelling at those who were poised to attack. With his help, they made it safely through the rest of the day's journey. As night fell, the bandit told Rosalind he would have to leave. Once again they found themselves outside another walled town where they would have to find "shelter" for the night. By now Jonathan was lapsing in and out of consciousness. His wounds were over thirty hours old, and in the brief moments that he was alert and awake, he knew they would have to be properly cleaned with antiseptic soon or gangrene would set in and he would surely die.

It looked increasingly as though Jonathan might die of something far speedier than gangrene, however. The crowd that gathered around the carts as they entered the town gate had become violent. Men and women were chanting, "Kill the foreigners," and even the smallest children were picking up rocks and hurling them at the group.

Somehow Jonathan managed to pull himself up to a sitting position. As he looked out over the hopeless situation, he suddenly heard a familiar name: "Ku-Mu-shih" (Pastor Goforth). Someone was calling his name in Chinese!

"I am here," he yelled back, watching intently as the crowd parted and two well-dressed young men emerged. Jonathan gave a cry of joy when he saw them. They were the two sons of one of his influential friends in Changte. He reached out his hand to greet them.

The taller of the two brothers climbed up on the cart and yelled at the crowd. "These people are good foreigners. They are friends of my father, and they work in Changte to bring happiness to our people. When I visited Changte last spring, this man took my father and me through his house, allowing me to look at everything he owned. Then he offered my father and me tea, and we talked for a long time together. We must offer him and his band the same hospitality," he said.

Jonathan was not sure exactly what position the young man held in the town. It must have been a respected one, because as soon as the young man said these words, the mood of the crowd completely changed. Now they could not do enough to help the missionaries. Jonathan and Dr. Leslie were gently carried into the inn and laid on the brick k'ang that served as the main bed.

Rosalind unwound the filthy, blood-incrusted bandages from around Jonathan's neck and left arm. She recoiled when she saw the gaping wound on the back of his skull. Jonathan knew it must look awful by now, but apart from bathing it in water, there was not much that could be done for it.

As Rosalind swabbed the stab wounds on her husband's arm with some warm water, there was a knock at the door, and the younger of the two brothers entered the inn. "This parcel was left for you by a party of engineers who came through two days ago, Ku-Mu-shih. That is how my brother and I knew to expect you." He held out a small bundle wrapped in linen cloth.

"Thank you," replied Rosalind as she unwrapped the bundle with trembling hands. She let out a gasp of delight and held up a dark brown medicine bottle. "Look, Jonathan!" she exclaimed. "It's a bottle of antiseptic liquid. Thank God! How did the engineers know we would be needing this!"

Jonathan smiled through cracked lips. "God has undertaken for us, my dear," he replied.

From his position lying beside Jonathan on the k'ang, Dr. Leslie oversaw the treatment of both of their wounds. The innkeeper brought Rosalind clean rags for bandages. It was amazing how much better everyone felt the following morning after a good night's sleep uninterrupted by shouts of violence or the fear that someone would creep in and slit their throats.

The two young brothers arrived at the inn early the next morning. They brought with them a hearty breakfast of millet gruel and fresh bread. While they all ate, the adults talked about the situation they found themselves in. Everywhere around them lay danger, but the only thing the missionaries could do in the face of it was to press on to Fancheng and from there try to make it to Hankow by boat. The older of the two brothers told the missionaries it was a good thing they had come as far west as they had, because two weeks earlier the empress dowager had sent a messenger to the south decreeing that all foreigners should be killed.

Jonathan stared at Rosalind, who met his eyes. "The messenger with the burnt feather!" she exclaimed.

Jonathan felt goosebumps rising on his unbandaged right arm as he realized just how close they had come to heading south. They would have been on a path to certain death if he had not changed his mind and decided to head in a westerly direction first.

"You must go on without delay," said the young man. "The entire country has gone mad. It is not safe for you to stay anywhere."

While Jonathan agreed in principle, he said, "But my son and Mr. Griffith—we don't know where they are." Tears flowed down his cheeks as he spoke, but he did not have the energy to wipe them away. Then the story of their lost son came tumbling out for the brothers to hear.

The two young men looked at each other. "My brother and I will do all we can to find them and send them after you, but you must not stop to wait for them. It is too dangerous," said the older brother, and then he bent his head close to Jonathan's ear. "It is better to lose one of your children than all of them," he whispered.

The words sent a chill down Jonathan's spine, but he had to admit the wisest thing for them to do was to press on in their journey.

The missionaries were all grateful when the brothers wrote a letter of introduction to the leader in the next town and sent along an official from their town to calm the crowds and give the missionaries safe passage until nightfall. The brothers also apologized for not sending any food or bedding with the travelers, explaining that it would only make them a target for robbery. The less they had with them, the more chance they would have of making it to Fancheng alive.

After warmly thanking the brothers, the band of missionaries left the town refreshed from a good night's sleep but daunted by what still lay ahead of them.

It was four in the afternoon when a runner caught up to the group. He brought good news for Jonathan and Rosalind. Paul had been found! Apparently he had been pulled away by the crowd when they were loading up to go. Mr. Griffith had seen that he was in trouble and had jumped off the cart to save him. Both of them had managed to get away and hide in an alley, but by the time their tormentors had stopped looking for them, the rest of the missionaries were long gone.

Eventually Mr. Griffith and Paul had found the cart and driver left behind for them, and they had started out on their own perilous journey twelve hours behind the others. Mr. Griffith and Paul had escaped any injuries and so were able to make faster progress. If all went well, the messenger said, they should catch up to the rest of the group after nightfall in the next town. Sure enough, later that evening Mr. Griffith and Paul finally caught up to the group. Both of them had cuts and bruises but otherwise were in good health.

The leader in the next town read the letter the brothers had written. At the urging of his wife, who was a Christian, he not only let the missionaries stay safely in his town but also sent them on their way the next day with a fully armed escort. The escort was to protect them all the way to Fancheng.

The missionaries continued on feeling a little safer, though the crowds that surged around them along the way were often angry and armed with rocks and sticks. At midnight two days later, they finally reached Fancheng. The first leg of their journey was over. Much to everyone's surprise, the engineers were waiting for them at the inn. They had hired several boats for the following night, hoping the missionaries would arrive in time.

After spending the day locked in a hot, filthy inn, everyone was relieved to climb aboard the boats for the ten-day trip downriver to Hankow. As Jonathan staggered aboard one of the boats, he was grateful that no matter what lay ahead, at least his family was together again.

Chapter 10

An Unexpected Response

The boats arrived at Hankow without incident, largely because the boat operators kept their craft near the middle of the river and ordered the foreigners to stay out of sight. Once they reached Hankow, though, they were unable to get permission to land and instead were ordered to continue on to Shanghai, where the Goforths would catch the first steamer available back to Canada.

Everyone was stiff and sore by the time the boats reached Shanghai. Jonathan, who had been able to rest a little on the trip downriver, regained a bit of his strength each day.

The Shanghai they stepped off the boat into that day was vastly different from the Shanghai they had passed through twelve years before. Refugees, both Chinese and foreign, many of them with dazed looks on their faces, walked the streets. The waterfront was filled with people clambering for tickets to leave the country. Women with tear-streaked faces begged, men slipped money over the counter, and children sat on steamer trunks staring silently ahead, obviously unable to take in the rapid changes that had overtaken their young lives.

Upon arrival, Jonathan headed straight for the Bank of Shanghai, where he had some money in a savings account. He withdrew it all, and the family ate well for the first time in nearly three weeks. In all the chaos, Jonathan was also able to find the family an unfurnished house to stay in and reserve boat passage to Canada in ten days' time.

When Rosalind finally put the last child to sleep on the floor their first night in Shanghai, she turned to Jonathan. "What are we going to do?" she whispered desperately. "Look at us. We are all dressed in rags. There's no way we can go back to Canada looking like this. None of us even has a change of clothes, and your shirt and pants are covered with blood."

Jonathan studied his wife and sleeping children. She was right. They looked like beggars, but where would they get suitable clothing for the trip home? Because of the Boxer Rebellion, there were few Western-style clothes for sale in Shanghai. They would have to buy fabric and make clothes for all six of them, but how could they do that in only a few days, and without a sewing machine?

The next morning there was a knock at the door, and two Chinese women stood outside. They explained that they had seen the Goforths' name on a refugee list, and although they had never met, the women had heard they were missionaries and wanted to help them. Maybe, they asked, there was some sewing they could do for the family?

Rosalind stood at the door for a full minute holding the women's hands and sobbing. In the midst of so much hatred, the kindness of these two visitors overwhelmed her. Before the week was out, the girls had dresses, petticoats, and warm overcoats, and Paul had pants and shirts and a jacket. But in all the activity, Rosalind had completely overlooked making anything for baby Wallace. By the time she realized this, it was too late. They had to board the ship with him wrapped in an old towel and a blanket. Rosalind had fabric to hand sew him a baby gown and bonnet, but by the time she had everyone settled in their cabin, she was too worn out to pick up a needle.

It was with mixed feelings that Jonathan and Rosalind Goforth stood watching the lights of Shanghai slip from view on the evening of August 1, 1900. They were leaving the country they loved so dearly. Now all they could do was pray for peace. Jonathan had barely had time to think about little Florence. He was shocked when he realized she had been dead only six weeks. He put his arm around his wife and laid her head on his shoulder. They would face the future together.

The ship crossed the East China Sea and three days later dropped anchor in Yokohama Bay, Japan. Jonathan and the three oldest children watched as a lighter boat came alongside and supplies were loaded onto the ship. An hour later, Rosalind joined them on deck with baby Wallace, now dressed in a well-made baby gown and hand-knitted cardigan.

"Oh, Jonathan!" exclaimed Rosalind before he had time to ask. "God provided for the baby. The lighter boat brought a package for us from Mrs. Edwards with the China Inland Mission. She must have stopped in Japan, too, on her way home. But how she knew we would be aboard this ship I don't know. Anyway, the package was filled with clothes, most of them baby clothes, just the right size for Wallace. Isn't that amazing. It's exactly what we prayed for!"

Jonathan smiled at his wife. It had been a long time since he had seen her so joyful.

When the Goforths arrived in Canada, they were greeted as celebrities. Many people had feared they would not make it out of China alive, and everyone clamored to hear the story of their escape.

Each day Jonathan searched the Canadian newspapers for news of China. He found both good and bad news. The good news was that the Boxer Rebellion had ended on August 14, 1900, just two weeks after the Goforths had left. The foreign powers with spheres of influence in China (Russia, Great Britain, Germany, France, Japan, and the United States) put together a force of nineteen thousand soldiers that was dispatched to retake Peking, home of the empress dowager Tz'u-hsi, who had actively encouraged the Boxers to kill foreigners and burn down Western churches and factories. The foreign troops were much better organized and equipped than the Boxers and Imperial Chinese soldiers. Within days they had captured Peking and forced the royal family to flee northward. An uneasy peace had settled over China, but it was not yet stable enough for missionaries to return. In the end, over two hundred fifty foreigners were killed by the Boxers, along with thousands of Chinese Christians.

While Jonathan waited for China to open, he filled his time in Canada by both telling the story of his family's escape from Changte and challenging everyone he came in contact with about the need for more missionaries to return to China as soon as the door to do so opened again.

It took over a year for the Chinese government and the foreign powers to negotiate the Peace of Peking settlement. This settlement gave everything to the foreign powers and nothing to China. China was required to pay out huge amounts of money in reparations, the foreign powers got more lenient trade arrangements, and the Chinese had to dismantle all their coastal defense facilities.

Jonathan was very concerned about the agreement. In his mind it wasn't a real agreement at all but was several large foreign powers bullying China into doing what they wanted. The agreement did not solve any of the problems caused by foreigners in China. In fact, it made them worse. It seemed to him only a matter of time before the whole problem exploded again and foreigners would once again be the target of hatred and violence. Deep in his heart, Jonathan knew the time to reach China was short. The Boxer Rebellion had been a powerful uprising, and while it had drawn attention to some problems, it had not solved them. In Jonathan's opinion the foreign powers were foolish to think things would ever go back to the way they were.

All of this made Jonathan eager to return to China. If the time was short, as he thought it was, he didn't have a day to waste! In mid-October 1901, the borders of China were once again opened to foreigners, and Jonathan was one of the first to go back. He left Rosalind in Canada with the children, including their new baby, Constance. Once he had checked things out, he would arrange for them to travel back to China to join him.

When Jonathan finally made it back to Changte, the church and his house were still standing, though both had been ransacked and nothing of value was left. As he walked around his old house wondering about the fate of his Chinese friends, Jonathan heard footsteps running though the courtyard. "Ku-Mu-shih, Ku-Mu-shih, is that you?" someone called.

Jonathan turned around, and there stood Mr. Ho, one of the leaders in the church before the Boxer Rebellion. The two men embraced each other.

"Mr. Ho! Praise God you are alive!" said Jonathan.

The two of them laughed and cried together.

"Tell me what happened to you after we parted," Jonathan asked.

Mr. Ho sat on the floor in the kitchen, and the expression on his face grew serious. Jonathan sat beside him. "Once you left," began Mr. Ho, "I decided to stay inside the church to protect it until you returned."

"But we begged you not to do that. We didn't expect you to risk your life to protect the church. Buildings can easily be replaced," said Jonathan.

"I know," replied Mr. Ho, "but I could not leave. This place carried the memory of you all, and all I wanted to do was protect it. However, I was not able to do so for long. On the second day, the city officials sent men to get me and take me to the court." He paused for a moment. "They dragged me through town, where a mob gathered to torment me. They spat and yelled that I should be cut into four pieces for following the foreign devils. Finally I was taken into the courthouse, and the mob stood outside the doors chanting. I was left alone in a room that had a window overlooking the crowd. What an opportunity it was! I told myself I could preach to over a thousand people at once. So I stood at the window and shared the gospel with the mob."

Jonathan reached out and patted Mr. Ho on the shoulder. "Good for you! How did the crowd respond?"

"They listened for a while and then started yelling at me again. They told me I must have been poisoned with foreign medicine and that I should be ashamed to follow the foreign devils' God. But I felt no fear," Mr. Ho said triumphantly. "God was with me. Soon I was taken before the magistrate, and he asked me why I had disgraced my whole family and even my country by following the God of the foreign devils."

"How did you reply?" asked Jonathan, pulling some bread from his bag and offering half of it to Mr. Ho.

"I said, 'Your honor, I am not following the foreigners. I am following the true and living God. This God loved us and sent His Son to die in our place so that He might save us from our sins and their consequences. The gods that I used to worship, and that you worship, are not gods at all. Before I became a follower of the true God I used to be an idol maker by trade. With my own hands I made those gods, large ones for people who could afford a lot of money, small ones for those who could not. But they did no good; they were merely pieces of wood. I had many gods in my home, yet they had no power to stop me from dishonoring my parents or make me obey the laws of the land. You yourself know that I have been sentenced in this courtroom many times and beaten for my lawlessness. But from the time God possessed my life, I have not been sentenced to a beating once.' You should have seen the magistrate when I finished. He didn't know what to say. Finally he said, 'Go home. I will protect you,' and then he dismissed me."

"Thank God!" replied Jonathan heartily. "And how has it been for you since then?"

"We have survived, though not without difficulties," responded Mr. Ho. "The bank refused to release the money you left for the church workers, but I was able to sell food and make enough to support myself and my family. One day I did get caught by a gang and I was hung by my thumbs in a tree and beaten with rods. They dared not leave me there to die because everyone had heard the magistrate say he would protect me."

A moment of silence passed between the two men, and then looking Jonathan in the eye, Mr. Ho said, "Ah, I have said enough of my troubles. What of you and your family? How did you fare once you left us? We heard rumors that you had all been killed in an ambush."

Jonathan told Mr. Ho all that had gone on since they had parted sixteen months before.

When the two of them had finished talking, they decided to visit all the Christians left in Changte. Jonathan was delighted by what he found. Even though many of them had been beaten and tortured, they were all alive and full of stories as to how God had been with them through their trials. Every Christian, even the newest ones, had been strong enough to stand against the hatred that had threatened to engulf them.

Jonathan was also delighted to find that after escaping with them to Shanghai, Mrs. Cheng had made it safely back to Changte, though she had been tortured. Like Mr. Ho, she had been hung from a tree with a rope tied around her thumbs and left to die. However, when the sun had gone down, some compassionate neighbors came and cut her down.

Tears welled in Jonathan's eyes as he listened to Mrs. Cheng's story of faith and survival. He marveled at her faithfulness. Not only had she saved the life of his daughter Ruth while they were fleeing, but in the face of so much death and danger, she had not wavered one bit in her commitment to God.

Soon the church was back in action, and the Christians of Changte began gathering together regularly for worship, prayer, and Bible study. During this time many new converts were added to the church.

As part of the terms of the Peace of Peking agreement, the Chinese government had agreed to pay back anyone for the loss of property destroyed or stolen during the Boxer Rebellion. Soon after Jonathan got back to Changte, an official letter arrived asking him to list everything that belonged to him or the church that was destroyed during the uprising, along with its value. Since most of the items had been bought in Canada and shipped over, Jonathan wrote the values for them in Canadian dollars. Much to his surprise, the money to replace his lost and damaged property eventually arrived in the mail. There was one problem though. In the time it had taken for the money to come, there had been a large fluctuation in the value of the Canadian currency against the Chinese currency. As a result,

Jonathan ended up receiving twice as much money as he had originally expected! He did not know what to do. He felt it was wrong to keep the extra money, but he was also realistic enough to know that if he sent it back to Peking, it would simply find its way into the pocket of some corrupt official.

After giving the matter much thought, Jonathan decided to spend the money on something that would benefit a number of the Chinese Christians who had been through so much themselves. He drew up plans for "Peace Village." This village, which would consist of many small cottages with individual garden plots, would be built on a square of ground close to the mission compound. Until now, most of the men who worked with the mission as schoolteachers, hospital assistants, and evangelists had to spend months at a time away from their families. Peace Village would change all that. Now a worker's wife and children could come and live in Changte with the worker for the cost of the upkeep of one of the cottages. Jonathan worked tirelessly on this project, and the village was soon finished and the first families moved in.

By the middle of 1902, everything was going well, and Jonathan decided that things had settled down enough for Rosalind and the children to rejoin him. He sent a telegram asking Rosalind to return, and she in turn telegraphed him back saying she and the children would be setting sail on July 1.

Jonathan was overjoyed. He set about making arrangements for their return, pre-enrolling Paul and Helen in the China Inland Mission school in Chefoo, and spring cleaning the entire house. As he worked, however, he began to notice he was feeling weaker and weaker. Then he became delirious. He was soon diagnosed as having typhoid fever, an often fatal disease. His life hung in the balance for many days before he began to make a slow recovery.

Many people might have become bored lying in bed day after day as they recovered, but not Jonathan Goforth. His body might be still, but his mind was whirling with activity. A plan was beginning to take shape in his head. After returning to Changte, the Presbyterian Council had divided the region around the city in three. It had put Jonathan in charge of the largest of these areas, which stretched from northeast of the city to the northwest. Since the work in Changte itself was in the capable hands of such workers as Mr. Ho and Wang-Mei, Jonathan's thoughts turned to this vast area. Lying in bed he decided the only way to evangelize the area properly was to take some workers and his family and spend about a month in each of the larger towns in the region. The men in the group would go throughout the town and surrounding countryside and preach the gospel while Rosalind would welcome the women into the courtyard of the house and preach to them there. Each evening they would hold a meeting to which all the men and women who were interested in hearing more could come. Jonathan could see it all in his mind. Rosalind would play the new portable organ she was bringing back with her from Canada, and there would be lots of hymn singing and testimonies given throughout the service.

After a month, the Goforths would move on to rent another house in another town, leaving one of the evangelists who had worked with them behind to nurture the new Christians. In this way Jonathan estimated he could start about ten new churches a year, taking two months out to visit the ones that were already established.

The more he thought about the plan, the more Jonathan liked it. He could see no reason for them to stay in Changte, not with all of the needs in the outlying areas.

During his bout with typhoid, Jonathan mailed several letters to Rosalind in Tientsin, where she was awaiting further instructions from him. The postmaster in Peking kept sending them back to Changte, thinking the Goforths were all back there together. No matter how the letters were addressed, he didn't seem to be able to grasp that Jonathan and Rosalind were in two separate places in China and writing to each other. As a result, Rosalind had been in China for almost a month with only a brief telegram to tell her Jonathan had typhoid. She had no way of knowing whether he was dead or alive, or if he would want her to come to him or keep the children away during the infectious stage of his disease.

By now Jonathan was missing his family a great deal. As soon as he was well enough to travel, he set out on the two-week journey to Tientsin to meet up with Rosalind and the children and escort them back to Changte. It had been ten months since Jonathan had seen his family, and when he finally arrived, they were all relieved to see him up and about.

Jonathan was bursting to tell Rosalind of his new plan to reach the whole area north of Changte. He waited until the children were in bed. "Rosalind," he began, "I believe I have found the best way to use the time we have left in China."

"Oh," smiled his wife, putting down her hand sewing. "I would love to hear about it. Tell me more."

As Jonathan launched into a description of the nomadic life he had planned out for them all, he watched Rosalind's face go pale. After a couple of minutes Rosalind held up her hand. "Stop, Jonathan. You can't be serious! This would be a great idea if it were just you and I, but we have young children to think about. What are we to do with them while we are gallivanting around the countryside? They're too young to go to the mission school like Paul and Helen."

"We'll bring them with us," Jonathan replied, taken aback by his wife's lack of enthusiasm. He clasped her hands in his and reassured her. "I know it will work."

Jonathan watched as tears streamed down Rosalind's cheeks. "But we have already left four children in graves in China. Jonathan, I could not bear to take my children into the countryside. You know how those people live. Smallpox, dysentery, and typhoid are all there. You should know that! The illness you just had would have killed a child. No! I can't do it. Little Constance isn't even a year old yet." Rosalind sobbed deeply. "Ask me to do anything else, but don't ask me to risk our children's lives!"

"But, dear," Jonathan replied tenderly, "they will be safe in the Lord's keeping because I'm sure it's He who is leading us to take this step. The safest place for our children is in the path of duty."

"I don't care. The children and I are not going with you, and that's final," Rosalind said. "I can't go through that again, and you shouldn't ask me to."

Jonathan did not know what to do. This was definitely an unexpected response.

Chapter 11

I Will Trust You

As much as Jonathan pleaded, he could not convince his wife to join in his new plan. This made him sad. He did not want to lose another child any more than Rosalind did, but he was convinced that no child of his would die if they all followed his new plan, which he was certain was God's new direction for them.

The Goforth family returned to Changte, where everyone, especially Mrs. Cheng, was excited to see them. Ruth still remembered how the old woman had saved her life during the Boxer Rebellion. Jonathan watched with dismay, however, as Rosalind put her plan to protect the three little children from infectious diseases into action. Rosalind had obviously had a lot of time to think about it while in Canada. She decided to give up most of her evangelizing work so that she could look after the children herself. There would be no more Chinese nannies, and on the odd occasion when it was necessary for Mrs. Cheng to watch over the children, she would be under strict instructions not to take them out of the house and definitely not to allow them to mix with Chinese children.

Rosalind's new plan greatly concerned Jonathan, though he understood that his wife was still grieving over the loss of Florence and believed she was doing the right thing to protect the other children.

Despite Rosalind's best efforts to shield the children from disease, two-year-old Wallace came down with dysentery. Rosalind became frantic and immediately sent for the mission doctor. Thankfully, Wallace was a tough little boy, and he did not die.

Once Jonathan could see that his son would live, he left Rosalind and the children behind in Changte and set off to open the first of his mission outstations. It was a successful month. Everything went better than Jonathan could have imagined, with two exceptions: There was no organ music for the services and no one to talk to the women.

By the time he left to return to Changte, Jonathan was hoping Rosalind had changed her mind and would come with him next time. However, he was not prepared for the news that awaited him when he got back to the mission compound. By now Wallace had made a full recovery, but Constance lay deathly ill with the same disease.

Her little body was limp and clammy, and she didn't smile when she saw her father.

"How long has she been like this?" Jonathan asked, trying not to sound shocked by what he saw.

"Three days," Rosalind replied. "The doctor comes every morning, but he says she is very young and has a particularly bad case." Her voice trailed off, and she wiped a tear from her eye before she went on. "Oh, Jonathan, what else can we do? I can't bear to lose another child."

"We can only pray," replied Jonathan with a sigh as he slipped to his knees. Rosalind joined him, and the two of them prayed for their baby daughter. When Jonathan opened his eyes, the child was not moving. He touched her forehead, which felt cold. "Rosalind, Constance has gone to a better place," he told his wife gently.

Rosalind looked at her daughter and began to cry uncontrollably. Her body convulsed with deep sobs for several minutes. Finally, she bowed her head once more and prayed, the tears still streaming down her cheeks. "O God, it is too late for Constance," she said, "but I will trust You. I will go where You want me to go, but please keep the rest of my children safe."

The following day Constance was buried beneath the tree at the back of the compound beside her two sisters. The date was October 13, 1902. Had she survived, it would have been her first birthday.

After the funeral, Rosalind began packing. From now on, she promised Jonathan, she and the children would travel with him wherever he went.

Their first trip was to Wuan, a city about twenty miles from Changte along a potholed and winding road.

"Stop, stop!" yelled Jonathan yet again as they made their way towards Wuan. He was walking behind the first of three carts, the one his wife and children were riding in. A band of dedicated church workers was traveling in the second cart, while the third cart was loaded with their equipment for the evangelistic campaign.

The cart driver stopped and climbed down wearily, followed by Rosalind, four-year-old Ruth and two-year-old Wallace. They stood on the side of the road while the men in the group lined up across the back of the cart.

"On the count of three," yelled Jonathan. "One, two, three, heave."

Each man put his shoulder under the cart to help lift it off the ground, pushing it forward at the same time.

"It needs to go higher," yelled Rosalind, and the men lifted the cart a little higher until it cleared the rock that had jammed under the back axle.

Rosalind and the children climbed back into the cart, which pulled forward a few feet while the men lifted the second and third carts over the same rock.

Progress was painfully slow, and the entire team was exhausted by the time they reached Wuan. No one, not even the children, had enough energy to eat, and as soon as they found lodging at an inn, they all collapsed onto a large k'ang. They slept soundly all night. When they awoke the next morning, they were covered with bruises and cuts from their journey. Jonathan wondered whether this rough start would lead his wife to change her mind about traveling with the children. She remained firm, however, assuring him that wherever he went she would follow him.

The travelers were just finishing breakfast the next morning when they heard a knock at the inn door. In walked a man escorted by three armed guards. The man, who was obviously a high-ranking official, bowed to Jonathan and Rosalind and introduced himself.

"Good morning," he said. "I am Mr. Yen, the chief city official. I have come to pay you a visit." Then he spotted the children and looked startled. "Surely you did not allow the children to travel from Changte in the carts I saw outside in the courtyard?" he asked. "I traveled that road only last month, and parts of it were nearly impassable."

Jonathan looked at Mr. Yen. "We are happy to visit your town using any transportation available to us. As a family we have traveled many hundreds of miles in carts," he said.

"Well, you will not come to my town in a cart again!" replied Mr. Yen indignantly. "No! No! Whenever you come here you must get word to me, and I will send my sedan chairs for you. You must also use them when you leave. If you do not accept my offer, I will take it as a great personal offense!"

Jonathan opened his mouth to protest, but Mr. Yen held up his hand. "No," he said. "You will come to my town in my sedan chairs or not at all."

Not wanting to insult Mr. Yen, Jonathan accepted his kind gesture, and the two men talked on for a while. The conversation proved to be most helpful. Mr. Yen suggested a place the group could rent for their evangelistic efforts. In return, Jonathan presented Mr. Yen with a Bible in Chinese.

Later that day, the group moved into their new "home." The Goforths had one room to themselves, which Rosalind did her best to make as comfortable as possible for her family. First she tacked two blue cotton curtains to the rafters, the first around the k'ang and the second around a corner at the far end of the room so that Jonathan could use the space as his "private study." Then she turned one windowsill into a dresser and the other into Jonathan's bookshelf. After this, she and Jonathan dragged thin straw mattresses off the cart and placed them on the floor for the children to sleep on. Jonathan also dispatched the cook to buy bricks to make a fireplace. There was no need for a chimney, since the Chinese custom was to trap the smoke inside the house, only opening the door to let it out when it became difficult to breathe. Within an hour, the family was settled into its new home.

Once the family was organized, Jonathan turned his attention to the large room where the evening meetings were to be held. He and the Chinese evangelists plastered the walls with large banners that had Bible texts written on them. An area at the front of the room was marked off for the preaching platform, and a powerful lamp was strung over the spot. Next the hymn scroll was set up to the left of the platform. This was a long roll of white cotton fabric onto which were handwritten the words to fifteen simple hymns. The portable organ was placed on the right side of the platform. Once these details were taken care of, Jonathan sent everyone out to find as many chairs and benches as they could for people to sit on. By nightfall, everything was in place and ready for the meetings that would begin the next day.

The following morning, Jonathan followed the same routine he had for many years. He arose at 5 A.M. and exercised vigorously for fifteen minutes to wake himself up. Following this, with a pencil and notebook beside him, he began an hour and forty-five minutes of Bible study. He had notes for hundreds of different sermons and lessons he had already preached and taught, but he liked to study and preach on a fresh passage from the Bible every day. Following Bible study he ate breakfast promptly at seven o'clock, after which came family devotions. From eight to nine o'clock he held a Bible study and prayer meeting with the rest of his team of evangelists and helpers.

By ten past nine that morning, the team was fanning out to various promising preaching spots around Wuan, and Rosalind had set up the courtyard to receive any women who wanted to come to hear her speak.

After a full day of preaching, the evangelists would all meet back together for dinner and prepare for the evening service. This was always a lively event. A new hymn was taught to the crowd each night, and Jonathan would then preach for one last time that day.

Things in Wuan went well. Many Chinese people were astounded to see Europeans back in the area, especially after so many foreigners had been killed by the Boxers. "What would make you come back?" they asked. "What is so important that you would risk your lives to tell us?" Jonathan eagerly explained to them exactly what was so important as to bring him back to China: the need to share the gospel.

One day Mr. Yen paid another visit to the group. With a serious look on his face he took Jonathan aside. "You must answer me a question," he said. "Tell me why this Bible you gave me has so much power. Before you gave it to me I often took money in exchange for rendering unjust decisions in court, but now it is very different. I read this book, and I find if I make an unjust decision I cannot sleep!"

Jonathan smiled and guided Mr. Yen by the arm. "Sit down, my friend, and I will tell you where its power comes from."

By the end of the month there were over twenty new converts in Wuan, and many other people were interested in hearing more about the God the missionary and his helpers spoke of.

Chapter 12

Chang-san

For the next few years the Goforth family criss-crossed North Honan, preaching and teaching the Bible wherever they went. Every six months or so they would return to Changte to see how the work was getting along there. It was during one of these visits that Jonathan first laid eyes on Chang-san.

As he was speaking in an evening service at the Changte church, Jonathan noticed an intelligent-looking young man about twenty years old. At the end of the meeting, when he gave the invitation for those who wanted to know more about Christianity to go to a side room, the young man was one of the first to respond. When Jonathan saw this, he made his way through the crowd to talk to him. He asked where the young man was from and why he had come to the side room. The young man introduced himself as Chang-san and said he was visiting from the nearby village of Hsiwen. He had been drawn to the service by the cheerful singing.

As Jonathan patiently explained the gospel to Chang-san, tears filled the young man's eyes. Chang-san explained that he wanted to become a Christian, but his father had made it very clear over the years that his sons were to have nothing to do with foreigners. Chang-san was reluctant to cross his father because he had a particularly bad temper. Indeed, the people of Hsiwen had given his father the nickname "Fury" because of his temper.

Jonathan talked to Chang-san about doing what he knew was right and letting God take care of things with his father. That evening Chang-san became a Christian convert. The next night and the night after that, he came back to services at the church, staying afterwards to talk to Jonathan about what he should do next. The night before Chang-san was due to go home, Jonathan encouraged him to tell his family that he had become a follower of the true and living God. Chang-san agreed that this was the right thing to do, but he was still a little afraid of how his father would react.

For the next ten days Jonathan prayed for Chang-san and waited anxiously to hear from him. On the eleventh day, just as darkness fell, a man staggered into the mission compound. His clothes were shredded and he had several nasty gashes on his face. In the glum of twilight, Jonathan couldn't recognize the man or know what he wanted. "What can I do for you?" he asked. "Do you need a doctor?"

"It is me!" exclaimed the man, taking a step closer to Jonathan.

"Chang-san?" Jonathan gasped, hardly able to believe this was the same young man he had counseled just days before.

"Yes, it is me, Ku-Mu-shih," he replied. "I have come to you for advice."

"Come in," said Jonathan. "I will wash your wounds and we can talk."

Jonathan guided his visitor to a chair in the kitchen and got a bowl of warm water. "How did this happen to you?" he asked as he dipped a clean cloth into the water.

Chang-san sighed. "I did as you told me to. As I walked back to my village, all I could think of were your words, 'Your first step in your new life must be to confess Christ before your own people.' I was very scared to do this on account of my father, and I put it off for many days. I did not meet with my friends or talk to my family, fearing they would ask me questions about my time in Changte. Finally, I could bear it no longer, so I threw myself at my father's feet, weeping and banging my head against the brick floor."

Jonathan squeezed out the cloth and placed it gently on Chang-san's eye. "Go on," he said, dreading what he would hear next.

"I could not stop weeping, and my father concluded that I had gambled away the family's money in Changte. He told me he knew I had done something I regretted and that I should confess it and it would be over with. 'No, no, you don't understand,' I told him. 'I have done nothing I regret, but I have done something you will not understand. That is the reason I am weeping. I am a Christian now. I heard a missionary in Changte, and he told me the amazing story about how God loves every man and woman.' Before I could say anything more, my father sprang from his chair. He grabbed me by the back of my neck and began pushing and kicking me. He shoved me out the door into the street, where a big crowd of neighbors had gathered. My father kept right on beating me, yelling to everyone, 'The foreigners have bewitched him!' "

"What did you do then?" Jonathan inquired anxiously.

"I tried to protect my head," continued Changsan, "but I didn't fight back. Eventually my father, who is getting older, began to run out of strength. He gave me one final kick and yelled, 'Renounce this foolishness. Curse the foreigners!' But I said, 'No, Father, you can do what you want to me, but I have made up my mind to follow the true God.' At this my father became more furious than he had been before. 'Get me a hatchet!' he yelled at the crowd. 'My son has dishonored the whole family. I will kill him now!' When no one went to get a hatchet, my father ran inside to look for one himself."

"What did you do then?" asked Jonathan, pouring a cup of tea for his guest.

"It was the strangest thing," said Chang-san, shaking his head. "There are no other Christians in my village, yet several of the older men pulled me to my feet and helped me to a neighbor's house. They made me hide under a pile of straw and said they would come and get me when my father's anger had subsided. Later that night they did come back. They reported that my father had not yet calmed down and that my best hope was to flee. So I crept from my neighbor's house, climbed over the wall, and hurried all the way to you."

"I am glad you did," replied Jonathan.

"This is my question, Ku-Mu-shih," said Chang-san, looking into the missionary's eyes. "What do you think the true God would have me do next?"

Jonathan sat for a moment, speechless. In front of him sat a new convert who had nearly been killed for following "step one" in his new Christian life and had come to ask what "step two" might be.

"I don't know what you should do next," Jonathan admitted. "You must stay here with us tonight, and tomorrow I will call all the mission workers together to discuss your situation."

The following morning Chang-san told his story to the gathered missionaries and church workers who had assembled in Jonathan's study. When he had finished, they decided on a plan of action. They would all go to Hsiwen the following day and preach in the streets there while Jonathan tried to meet with Chang-san's father and talk to him about his reaction to his son.

Early the next morning they all set out for Hsiwen. Chang-san stayed behind in Changte because they all agreed that he would be in great danger if he went back with them.

The group's welcome in Hsiwen was less than cordial. No one showed any of the normal Chinese good manners when a visitor arrived in town. No chair was brought for any of them to sit on after their ten-mile walk, and no drink was offered. Undaunted, the Christian workers took up various positions around the town and began preaching. A few stray dogs and barefoot children stopped to listen, but not one single adult.

Jonathan paid a young boy to deliver a note to Chang-san's father asking him to come and visit later in the day. No reply came, and finally around lunchtime the missionaries met together. They agreed that preaching was not working, and they decided to sing choruses and hymns to see if that would attract more attention. They started by singing a rousing version of "Jesus Loves Me."

Slowly, as they sang, the mood of the village began to change. First one or two and then groups of adults began to linger near the missionaries and evangelists. Then a small group of men sat down to listen. One man dragged a table from a nearby courtyard and offered it to the missionaries to put their Bibles on. Another man carried out two benches for them to sit on, and an old woman produced a pot of tea and several small cups. Throughout the rest of the day the growing crowd listened attentively as the gospel was preached.

Jonathan, however, became concerned when Chang-san's father did not reply to his note. After all, the goal in visiting Hsiwen was to try to make it safe for Chang-san to return home. At three o'clock in the afternoon, Jonathan decided to pay Chang-san's father a visit, with or without an invitation.

When he arrived at the Chang family home, Jonathan learned that Mr. Chang had been warned that a foreigner was coming his way and had run out the back door of the house and hidden. There would be no talking to him today, but a crowd of Chang-san's relatives had gathered to look at the man who had "cast" a powerful "spell" over a member of their family. Jonathan decided it was an opportunity too good to miss. He invited the relatives to sit down, and right there where Chang-san had been beaten only three days before, he shared the gospel. It was late in the afternoon before Jonathan rejoined the rest of the missionaries and church workers for the long, dusty walk back to Changte.

A few days later, Chang-san heard from a friend in Hsiwen that many people there had been impressed by the missionaries' visit and that his father had calmed down enough for him to return home.

Jonathan insisted that Mr. Ho accompany Chang-san in case things did not work out with his father. It was just as well he did. When Mr. Chang saw his son again, he became enraged and began ranting. He grabbed a heavy iron poker and rushed forward to attack his son. Quickly Mr. Ho jumped between them and managed to wrestle the poker from Chang-san's father. He then held Mr. Chang's arm behind his back until he promised not to try to harm his son again. When Mr. Chang promised, Mr. Ho released his grip.

In China, giving your word was a very serious matter, and so Mr. Ho left Chang-san with his father, confident that the young man would not come to any physical harm. Over the next few weeks, missionaries and church workers visited Hsiwen several times to keep an eye on the situation and to continue preaching. As a result of the visits and Chang-san's urging, many people in the village became Christians, including all of Chang-san's immediate family except his father.

Finally, overcome at the changes he saw in so many of his family members, Mr. Chang decided to become a Christian himself. From that day on, he was a different man. Instead of cursing, now he sang choruses as he worked. He read his Bible aloud every morning and was so kind to the children of the village that they stopped calling him "Fury" and instead treated him like a kindly grandfather.

Chang-san and his younger brother, who had also become a Christian, asked their father for permission to join the evangelistic team in Changte. Even though this meant he would have to go without many of the things his sons provided for him, Mr. Chang encouraged them to go. "All Chinese people should hear of the one true God," he told them. "If He can change an old angry man like me, He is a God of much power."

There was one person in Hsiwen, though, who was not at all impressed with Mr. Chang's conversion, or anyone else's, for that matter. Her name was Mrs. Chang, and she was a great-great aunt of Chang-san. As the oldest woman in the Chang family, her opinions were greatly respected. She became furious when she learned that the younger members of the family were dishonoring their family gods and becoming Christians. She set about to make life as difficult as she could for the growing band of Christians in the village.

One day, on another visit to Hsiwen, Jonathan and Rosalind sat visiting with Chang-san's parents when his mother burst into tears. "I do wish we could reach old Mrs. Chang; she is so old and bitter. She hates all the Christians here. Everyone is scared of her tongue-lashings, and so they try not to displease her," she said through her tears.

Jonathan looked at his wife. He knew a Chinese woman would not welcome a man into her home. Rosalind looked back and smiled. "I know!" she said, and then turning to Mrs. Wang, one of the church workers, she said, "Go over to Mrs. Chang's house and ask her if I might visit her. We will stay here and pray while you are gone."

Mrs. Wang hurried off to see if the old woman would let a foreign woman with man's feet into her home. She arrived back at Chang-san's parents' house an hour later. "She says you are to come," she reported to Rosalind excitedly.

Jonathan smiled at his wife. "This time you go and I will pray for you," he said.

An hour later Rosalind burst back into the room. "Quickly, Jonathan, help me find a red and blue pencil, a fountain pen, and my writing pad."

Jonathan, who had been sitting reading his Bible, jumped up. "What do you need them for?" he asked as she rummaged around in the bottom of a leather bag.

"Mrs. Chang and I got talking about all of the pictures of gods she has tacked to her walls," Rosalind began as she pulled a writing pad from the case. "I asked her if she thought their eyes really watched what she was doing. She replied, 'Yes, of course they do. See how lifelike they look.' So I told her, 'What if I could make something that looked that lifelike? Would I have made a god? Would it see everything you do?' 'Ha,' she laughed at me. 'You couldn't do it! No human could make something that lifelike unless it had the spirit of a god inside it.' So I told her to wait and I would show her."

Jonathan helped his wife collect the last few items she needed and wished her well. He waited anxiously until nightfall when she returned.

"You should have seen her, Jonathan!" Rosalind exclaimed, her eyes shining brightly. "I drew a portrait of Mrs. Chang herself, and God helped me to give her the most lifelike eyes. When I showed it to Mrs. Chang, she was shocked. 'Give that to me!' she demanded, grabbing at the picture. But I said, 'No, not until you agree that this picture has eyes that seem to see, yet it is merely a picture I drew myself, right in front of you.' 'I agree,' she said. 'It is just as lifelike as the gods I have, but it is only a picture.

Just give it to me.' So I gave it to her, and she was happy. Really, Jonathan, I think she is just a lonely old lady. She says she is waiting to die and even has her coffin ready outside the bedroom door. She invited me to come back and talk with her some more. I think that's a good sign, don't you?"

"Indeed I do," replied Jonathan, smiling at his wife.

From then on, whenever the Goforths were visiting Hsiwen, they made a special point of going to see Mrs. Chang. At first she was not interested in discussing religious matters with them, but gradually her heart softened, until one day she too declared she wanted to become a Christian.

From that time on, the old woman completely changed. She owned a second house in town that she rented cheaply to the church so that they could start a school. Every Sunday she opened her courtyard and served tea to the women who wanted to meet for Bible study between church services. She even gave her coffin to the pastor, who for many years used it as a Bible and hymnbook stand.

Every time Jonathan came to preach in the church at Hsiwen, he saw the coffin and thought of old Mrs. Chang and how his wife's artistic abilities had helped convince her that it was useless to worship a drawing on a piece of paper.

Chapter 13

New Directions

The years rolled by, and in the spring of 1907 Jonathan was asked to accompany Dr. MacKay, secretary of foreign missions for the Presbyterian Church in Canada, on a trip to Korea. The three-week trip was an eye-opening experience for Jonathan. Christian revival was spreading across Korea at the time, and many Christian schools, churches, and hospitals were being built and staffed by thousands of new converts. Jonathan had experienced good results during his nineteen years of missionary work in China, but nothing like what he was seeing in Korea.

On their way back to China, Dr. MacKay and Jonathan traveled through Manchuria. While there, they visited three mission stations, all of which

Jonathan spoke at. He did not preach one of his prepared sermons but rather spoke about the revival and what he had seen in Korea. His enthusiasm was contagious, and when he had finished speaking, he was invited to return to the mission station to hold ten days of meetings. At the second station, the same invitation was extended, as well as at the third.

Jonathan had more than enough work to do in North Honan, but after receiving three identical invitations, he decided he had better think seriously about going back to Manchuria. He discussed the invitations with the Presbyterian Council in Honan province, and the council agreed to release him for a month in the fall. The response to the meetings in Manchuria was more than Jonathan could have hoped for. Everywhere he spoke, people began to weep and cry out to God to forgive their sins. Bandits knelt beside government officials and prayed for each other. Beggars and college students sat together all night discussing how the God of love had changed their lives.

Word of the success of the meetings spread like wildfire, and by the time Jonathan got back to make his report to the Presbyterian Council in Honan, the council had already heard. Over the next few weeks, letters began to pour in to the council from all over China. In the letters, other missionaries and church leaders pleaded with the council members to release Jonathan from his regular mission duties so that he could visit their mission station or church to share the same message he had shared in Manchuria.

By the spring of 1908, one year after Jonathan's trip to Korea, the Presbyterian Council decided that Jonathan Goforth's place was not just in the mission in Honan but was in the entire country. Jonathan was commissioned to hold meetings across China.

This new venture would involve many days of grueling travel to get to the various places where he was invited to speak. As a result, the Presbyterian Council decided it would be impossible for Rosalind and the children to accompany him, especially since Rosalind had given birth to two more children, Mary and Fred, following Constance's death. Reluctantly, Jonathan accepted the decision, and arrangements were made for his family to return to Canada for an extended furlough.

A few days before Rosalind and the children were due to leave, Rosalind and Jonathan took a long walk together. When they were alone, Rosalind turned to Jonathan and asked him a serious question. "Suppose when I got back to Canada I was stricken with an incurable disease and had very little time left to live. If I cabled you to come to me, would you?" she asked.

Jonathan looked at his wife of twenty years. "Rosalind," he replied, "you are asking me to make a decision about a situation that has not occurred and that I hope never will."

"But," his wife persisted, "would you come?"

Jonathan sighed deeply. He did not want to hurt his wife's feelings, but he knew she would not give up until he answered her. He had been called to China, and he would not let anything, not even someone he loved as dearly as her, come between him and that call. He hesitated for a moment, trying to think of a gentle way to tell her this. Then it came to him. "Rosalind," he began. "Suppose our country was at war with another and I was the commander of a very large and important unit. Would you think it right of me to desert my post even if I received a telegram that you were in the condition you suggested?"

He waited quietly for an answer. With tears streaming down her face, Rosalind looked up at him. "No," she said quietly. "Your duty would lie with king and country."

Jonathan reached for his wife's hand and held it tightly. He was grateful she understood the path that lay ahead for both of them.

For the next year, Jonathan Goforth crisscrossed China. Everywhere he spoke, large numbers of Chinese people became Christians. He was often at the point of exhaustion because the large crowds that attended his meetings would not let him stop preaching. Sometimes a single meeting would go on for twelve hours or more, ending only when it became too dark to see the front of the room!

By 1909 it was long past time for Jonathan to go on furlough, so he returned to Canada to be reunited with his family. Following a joyful reunion, Jonathan spent the next ten months traveling around Canada with Rosalind and their six children. A number of churches welcomed him as he shared with them about the revival meetings in China and Manchuria. Many other churches, though, did not invite him to speak. They didn't want to risk an all-day meeting breaking out in their orderly midst!

While it was good to be together in Canada, the Goforth family longed to be back in China. It was a great relief to them when they were finally given permission to return in June 1910. The World Missionary Conference was to be held in Edinburgh, Scotland, that month. Since Jonathan was chosen to represent the Canadian Presbyterian Church at it, the family would travel to China via Great Britain. After the conference in Scotland, Jonathan was invited to Spurgeon's Tabernacle in London for a ten-day speaking engagement. He was also invited to speak at the huge Keswick Convention. Both of these events brought thousands of people to hear Jonathan speak. As he looked out on the faces of people eagerly listening to what he had to say, Jonathan felt a twinge of sadness that the British seemed more ready to listen to his message than people in his homeland.

The Goforth family finally arrived back in China in August 1910. Upon the family's arrival, the Presbyterian Council decided to split Jonathan's time between holding revival meetings across China and working in North Honan province. The plan, which required a great deal of responsibility, had one problem: Jonathan had no Chinese evangelists or preachers to work alongside him.

Over the years, Jonathan had trained fifteen Chinese men as evangelists, all of whom were busy at work in their own mission fields or were working with other missionaries. Jonathan didn't have the heart to ask any of them to leave the good work they were doing and come back to work with him. Instead, he prayed and asked God to give him a new man to work alongside him. He did not immediately recognize the answer to his prayers when he saw the man. No one could blame him; there was hardly a less likely candidate for an evangelist than Su Chuangting.

In November a huge tent was set up in the center of Changte as part of a special evangelistic campaign. Jonathan preached there three times a day for twenty-nine days straight. Many people were converted during the campaign, and on the last night, over a thousand people were jammed into the tent.

As the final service started, Rosalind played the organ and eleven-year-old Wallace accompanied her on the violin. While they played, from his perch on the platform at the front, Jonathan watched as a rickshaw pulled up to the back of the tent and a well-dressed man climbed out. The man steadied himself against the wheel for a moment while he reached into his pocket to pay the driver. Jonathan was sure he had not seen this man before and hoped he was coming into the tent. That is, until the man turned around and began staggering down the center isle. Every eye turned to watch the disturbance as Su Chuangting fumbled his way to the very front row and plunked himself down.

Jonathan's heart sank. The man was obviously very drunk. Even from six feet away Jonathan could smell the liquor on Su Chuangting's breath. As the last lines of the hymn were sung, Jonathan prayed that the drunken visitor would not disrupt the service. He then stood and began to preach on the verse "This is a faithful saying, and worthy of all acceptation, that Jesus Christ came into the world to save sinners" (1 Timothy 1:15).

As Jonathan preached about sin, Su Chuangting became very agitated. He muttered angrily to himself and kept rising to his feet as if he were going to walk out, but he didn't. The service lasted a long time, and by the end of it, some of the effects of the alcohol on Su Chuangting had worn off. When Jonathan invited those who believed the message he had just preached to raise their hands, Su Chuangting's hand shot into the air. Later that night, after the service was over, Su Chuangting asked Jonathan how he knew so much about him and the sins he had committed. "At first I was humiliated that you were telling everyone all the sins I had committed, but then when I heard that God would forgive me, I forgot about my humiliation and I wanted to know Him," Su Chuangting said.

The following morning, right after breakfast, there was a knock at the door. When Jonathan answered it, Su Chuangting was standing there. He started talking before he was invited in. "Pastor," he said excitedly. "My father is a noted Confucian scholar from one of the proudest families in the province. When I told him what I had done last night he flew into a rage. He began slapping my face, and then he ordered me out of the house. My wife spat on me and told me she no longer wanted to live with me, and when I went to my job as secretary of the electric-light company, I was told I had been dismissed."

Jonathan wasn't sure what to say to comfort the man. "I am so sorry…" he began.

"No, no," interrupted Su Chuangting. "I am not here for pity. Something happened to me last night, and I must get to the bottom of it. You must take me with you everywhere you go! I want to learn the secret of how it is possible that last night as I prayed my whole past life seemed to drop off me like a cloak. Now I have no desire to drink or go with prostitutes or smoke tobacco or do any of the other things that bound me so strongly." He grasped Jonathan's hand. "I am going to follow you all over the world, even if I have to starve for it. I have to learn the secret of the power that has brought about this amazing change in me. The things I once hated I now love. During the Boxer Rebellion, I so hated you and all foreigners that if I could have gotten near you with a knife, I would have killed you. Now, somehow, I feel I would gladly die for you!"

Jonathan was astounded. Could this man be the new worker he had prayed for?

The two men talked for a long time as Jonathan explained to Su Chuangting what it would be like to travel with him. There would be few home comforts, they would walk for many hours each day, people would spit and throw rocks at them, and sometimes they would go hungry. Jonathan made the missionary life sound as grim as he possibly could, but it did not deter Su Chuangting. When Jonathan had finished, Su Chuangting was still eager to go with him. "I will go and get my belongings from my house," he told Jonathan, "and this afternoon I will be ready to follow you wherever you go."

That is exactly what he did. Indeed, Su Chuangting turned out to be an intelligent student. Within a year he was a very popular and powerful speaker. He worked tirelessly alongside Jonathan. The two men worked together for five years until Jonathan's health began to deteriorate.

By mid-1915, Jonathan was so weak and ill that he had to be admitted to the hospital. His doctor warned him sternly. "Mr. Goforth," he said, "do not return to Changte to work. If you do, you will be committing suicide as surely as if you were to take an overdose of opium."

Jonathan took the doctor's advice and returned to Canada with his family to regain his strength. By now Jonathan was fifty-six years old and Rosalind was fifty-one. No one would have blamed them for retiring, but that word was not in Jonathan Goforth's vocabulary! There was work to do, and while he still had breath, he would do it.

The Presbyterian Mission Board in Canada would not give Jonathan permission to return to Changte to live, even though he was the founder and leader of all the Presbyterian mission work in Honan province. The climate in Changte was harsh, and they feared Jonathan would become sick again. They suggested the Goforths find a place with a more temperate climate to settle in. Eventually Jonathan decided on Kikungshan, located on a high plateau about three hundred miles south of Changte. It was a popular health resort destination and had a temperate climate year-round.

The Goforths returned to China to set up their new home. They planned on spending several quiet months settling into their new surroundings, but a week after arriving, Jonathan received an urgent request that he could not refuse. The request came from General Feng Yu-Hsiang, a man Jonathan had heard about but had never met. General Feng had been a nineteen-year-old soldier during the Boxer Rebellion. At that time, he had vehemently believed that all foreigners should be killed and had followed up his beliefs with action. In the city of Paotingfu, his company of soldiers, along with a mob of Boxers, had been responsible for the massacre of an entire group of American Board missionaries and their children, along with all the Chinese Christian converts in the area. Later the same summer, the company had participated in the torching of a house in southern Honan province in which a number of Presbyterian missionaries and their children had perished.

Of all the many deaths General Feng witnessed during the Boxer Rebellion, two incidents related to the massacre of the missionaries disturbed him the most. When he thought back to the killing of the American Board missionaries in Paotingfu, he remembered one missionary, whose name he later learned was Miss Morrell. She had stood outside the mission compound gates pleading with the mob of soldiers and Boxers to kill her and spare the lives of the other missionaries. In the end, the mob showed no mercy and killed all the missionaries. Over the years, as General Feng thought back to this event, he could not fathom the faith and courage of someone who was willing to die in the place of her friends. He knew he did not have friends who would be that loyal to him, and he began to ask himself where that kind of fearless love came from. And at the burning of the Presbyterian mission house, General Feng had watched in amazement as the missionary occupants of the house were overcome with fire and smoke. None of them were frantic; none of them panicked. One image was etched in his memory from that day. On the upstairs veranda, a father had stood tenderly holding his young son as the two of them waited to die in the flames. The father seemed so at peace as he comforted his son. Again General Feng wondered where the kind of peace the father displayed came from.

After the foreign powers had stepped in to end the Boxer Rebellion, General Feng found himself becoming more and more disturbed by the images of those dying missionaries and the questions their deaths had raised in his mind. Eventually, in 1911, he heard of a large Christian gathering being held by an American named John R. Mott. General Feng went to the gathering looking for answers to his questions about the amazing behavior of these Christians in the face of death. He left the meeting a Christian convert. From that day on, General Feng spoke out boldly about his new faith. He quickly became well respected for his moral values and his fairness both by the men who served under him and by his superiors.

Now General Feng had sent a messenger to Jonathan asking him to speak to the thousands of soldiers under his command. The army was stationed about three days' journey south in a hot region of the country just beyond the Yangtze River. It was not a good time for such an invitation to arrive. China was in the grip of a searing summer, and the Goforths were even feeling its effects up in their new home. But worse than the thought of going to the hot valleys was the news that cholera had broken out down there. Still, Jonathan did not hesitate for a moment. The opportunity was too good to miss, and so the Goforths packed their bags and went to meet General Feng and his army.

When Jonathan met General Feng for the first time, the general told him about his conversion and how thousands of members of the army, along with their wives and children, were becoming Christians.

During one of the services with the soldiers, Jonathan turned to the general, who was seated on the platform next to him, and asked, "General Feng, would you tell us what you were like nine years ago before you trusted yourself to the Lord Jesus Christ?"

General Feng jumped to his feet. "I was a devil back then," he began. "I had a demon temper. Even if an officer offended me, I would yell at him and box his ears. At that time my men all hated me, and I know they would have stuck a knife in me if they had the opportunity. Then Jesus Christ came into my heart and took control. His divine love took over. Since then I have ruled with love and not my bad temper, and I assure you tonight that all my men would die for me."

The assembled men cheered, and Jonathan could see the love they had for their leader.

It had been arranged for Jonathan to speak at two meetings a day for ten days, and General Feng expected all one thousand of his officers to be in attendance at the meetings. By the end of the visit, Jonathan had baptized five hundred seven army officers, along with hundreds of women and children. The Goforths returned to their new home greatly encouraged and ready to take on the next challenge that came their way.

Although Jonathan and Rosalind's official address was Kikungshan, they continued their nomadic life, spending an average of five days at a time in any one place. General Feng invited them back to speak to his troops again, and all in all, over four thousand soldiers were baptized as a result of Jonathan's preaching.

In the summer of 1920, the Goforths faced a difficult challenge. The whole of North-Central China was experiencing a devastating famine. Between thirty million and forty million people were starving to death. All of the missionaries in the area put aside their other work and did their best to alleviate people's suffering in any way they could.

Jonathan went to Changte to help out, but Rosalind was too sick to go with him. It was only later that Jonathan found out how his wife had played a part in saving thousands of lives. Rosalind had been desperately searching for some way to help with famine relief when it came to her that she should write an appeal letter for funds. She wrote a single page, outlining the information she had been given by various foreigners who had come to Kikungshan for health reasons. She then took the letter to a neighbor, who had a mimeograph machine, and had one hundred fifty copies made. She visited all the foreign missionaries staying nearby and handed out copies of the letter. Within twenty-four hours, Rosalind's letter had been translated into at least ten languages and sent out around the world.

Money for famine relief began to flow in from all over the globe. Rosalind herself received over one hundred twenty thousand dollars to go to famine relief, and many other missionaries were sent that much or more. All in all, Rosalind's one-page letter, written in less than half an hour, saved tens of thousands of lives. It did something else, too. It opened the hearts of many Chinese people to the message the missionaries had come to share.

Of course, Jonathan was determined to make the most of this openness. He planned an extensive tent campaign throughout the entire Changte area. Rosalind went with him. By then it was early winter, and together they braved icy-cold conditions to get the gospel message out. They slept in old huts, with the wind howling through the cracks in the walls and the rain trickling through the roof. Jonathan felt that every hardship was nothing compared to the joy of leading over three thousand people to faith in Christ during those winter months.

In the summer, Jonathan was invited back to speak to General Feng's army. He was eager to speak to them again and delighted to read what the local newspapers said about the soldiers. One Chinese reporter wrote:

> *Other soldiers when they came seized our houses and public buildings and made off with anything they took a fancy to, and our wives and daughters were at their mercy so that the people called them the soldiers of hell. Now General Feng leads his men through the city and nothing is disturbed and no one is molested. Even the General lives in a tent, as his men do, and everything they need they buy, and no one is abused. The people are so delighted they call them the soldiers of heaven.*

Jonathan couldn't have been happier when he read this report and many others like it. He always preached that the gospel had the power to change lives, and now many people in China were able to see that life-changing power at work for themselves. In a letter home he wrote, "I am sixty-five today....Oh, how I covet, more than a miser his gold, twenty more years for this soul-saving work."

Jonathan did not know, however, that on the other side of the Pacific Ocean the Presbyterian Foreign Missions Board was making decisions that would affect the rest of his life. It was not until he got home to Canada on furlough that he found out what those decisions were.

Chapter 14

Manchuria

Back home in Canada, Jonathan Goforth once again set out on a daunting round of meetings, over four hundred of them. At these services many people would ask him, "Are you going to retire?" Jonathan's reply was always the same. "I'm not going to sit in a rocking chair and wait to die, not while there is work to be done!"

The Presbyterian Foreign Missions Board, however, was not in good financial shape. It was over $166,000 in debt and was looking for ways to save money. One money-saving idea it came up with was to combine much of its missionary work in China with the work of other missions. This plan not only reduced the total number of missionaries serving in the field but also cut down on how many mission stations it needed to support. It was decided that the North Honan region, which included the Changte area, would be blended into this new combined mission that was to be called the Union Mission.

Almost overnight, Jonathan no longer had a role to play in the region that had been his home and base of work for so many years. Still, not willing to give up his missionary work, the now sixty-five-year-old white-haired Canadian searched for another way to go back to China. Eventually he was able to persuade the Presbyterian Foreign Missions Board to let him return to China and try to establish a new mission in an area where no other missionaries were working. Because the political situation in China was still very unstable, the board left it up to Jonathan to decide where this would be once he had returned.

For the next two years, Jonathan and Rosalind Goforth traveled around China conducting evangelistic meetings and looking for a permanent base for their mission work. No matter how hard they tried, they could not seem to find a permanent home. Each time they thought they had finally found a place to settle, a door would close, and they would be forced to look for another location.

Finally, late in 1926, Jonathan received a letter from the Irish Presbyterian Mission in Newchwang, Manchuria, asking him to consider moving to that region to work. The letter said that because of the political uncertainty in China and the vast resources of the area, millions of Chinese people had poured north into Manchuria over the past year.

Manchuria lay at the extreme northeast tip of China and was flanked in the south by the Yellow Sea, Mongolia in the west, and Russia and Korea in the north and east. Russia and Japan had both tried to exert their influence over the region, with the Russians building a railroad across the area in an attempt to open up the remote and sparsely populated areas and spread their influence. By 1926, Russian influence had waned, leaving Japan alone in trying to exert her influence over the area. Much as had happened in the American West with the railroad, people followed the railway into Manchuria seeking land on which to live and farm. As they did so, villages and towns began to spring up along the route of the railroad. The railroad also allowed missionaries access to parts of Manchuria where they had never been before.

Jonathan was aware that many people back in Canada thought he was crazy for even considering moving into Manchuria, and they had written to tell him so. They reminded him that he was nearly seventy years old and his wife was weak from constant illness. It was not possible for one old man and a sick wife to make inroads in Manchuria with the gospel message. Jonathan did not listen to their concerns. He was convinced that Manchuria was where God wanted him to be.

Not everyone had concerns. Some people were inspired by the challenge before Jonathan. One young graduate of Knox College in Toronto, Allan Reoch, joined Jonathan and Rosalind, as did two young women, Annie Kok from Holland and Nancy Graham from New Zealand. Jonathan was encouraged having these young people with him. They were so willing to go into Manchuria, though he knew the bulk of the early work would fall to him, since none of the three was proficient at speaking Mandarin Chinese.

Finally, January 23, 1927, the day the band of five missionaries was to board the train for Manchuria, arrived. Jonathan had checked Rosalind out of the local hospital earlier in the morning. Rosalind sat quietly in a chair on the station platform waiting for the train to arrive. She was sixty-two years old and very frail and had lost over fifty pounds, yet she was as enthusiastic as the others about opening up a new mission field.

That winter proved to be one of the coldest on record, and when they arrived in South Manchuria, a blizzard hit. Jonathan had never experienced such cold weather anywhere, not even in his native Canada. Despite the freezing cold, everyone's spirits remained high as the train pulled in to the station at Changchun. Jonathan, Rosalind, and the two young women were going to stay in Changchun while Allan Reoch went on alone to Szepingkai to look for a permanent home for them all.

As they waited, Jonathan read the newspapers each day and waited anxiously for letters from their old friends in China. Every scrap of news he received seemed to be worse than the last. By all accounts, China had once more fallen into a state of civil war, and again foreigners were an easy target. Most mission societies were pulling their missionaries out of the country, and those who stayed were warned that they were staying at their own peril.

While things were a little more politically stable in Manchuria, there was always the possibility that the unrest to the south could spill over into the region. And then there was the constant threat from the Japanese, who were always looking for some situation or another that they could use to help extend their influence in Manchuria. Eventually Jonathan received a letter from the British consul in Mukden (also known as Shenyang) ordering all British subjects to pack their bags and be ready to flee the area immediately if they received word to do so.

One by one letters arrived telling Jonathan that all of the other places where he had tried to settle and start a new work had been closed to foreigners. He was glad to be in Manchuria, where so far missionaries had been allowed to stay and work.

Eventually news came from Allan Reoch that he had found a perfect place to rent. It was located on one of the main streets of Szepingkai and was large enough to house the missionaries and provide space for a meeting hall. There was just one problem: The rent was high, and the owner insisted on being paid a year's rent in advance.

Jonathan was unsure what to do. On the one hand, the British consul was telling them to be ready to evacuate the area at any moment, yet here was a building that sounded ideally suited to their needs. What should he do? Should he spend the money to secure it? And what if he did that and they were told to evacuate? The mission board would be out of pocket a large sum of money.

After a night of prayer, Jonathan decided to send a telegram to Allan Reoch telling him to go ahead and rent the place and the four of them would join him there. On April 28, 1927, Jonathan, Rosalind, Annie Kok, and Nancy Graham arrived in Szepingkai. Everyone went straight to work preparing the place. Jonathan also wrote to Su Chuangting, his old friend and helper, asking if he would come to Manchuria to help preach to the millions of people who had never heard the gospel.

At the beginning of May, the missionaries began services in their new meeting hall. By the end of May, everything was going better than Jonathan could have hoped. There had been no order from the British consul telling them to flee, and men and women were pouring into the meeting hall to hear him preach. On an average, twelve people a day were becoming Christians, and by June 1, two hundred new members had been added to the church.

Jonathan was glad when Su Chuangting finally arrived to help him. He knew, however, that a lot more could be done in reaching the people of Manchuria with the gospel if he just had more workers. He wrote to the Presbyterian Foreign Missions Board in Canada about the wonderful opportunities that existed. He hoped his words would stir them to send him more workers. In his letter he said, "You can imagine our joy at seeing about two hundred decisions during the month of May.... We haven't the shadow of a doubt but that the results we have seen here during May might have been seen in dozens of other centers in our new field had it been possible for our little band to be in other centers at the same time."

While Jonathan waited eagerly for a reply, he began to make preparations for the new missionaries he was certain would soon be sent to join him. After all, Manchuria was the perfect place to work for the many missionaries who had been ordered out of other parts of China.

Finally a reply came from Canada, but it was not the wonderful news Jonathan had been expecting. Yes, the Presbyterian Foreign Missions Board appreciated the opportunities in Manchuria, and yes, it did support the Goforths in their work. However, there was no plan or money to send any more missionaries to help with their work.

The entire group was stunned by the response. It was as if they were standing in a huge field of ripe grain and the farmer would not send anyone to help them harvest it before winter set in. Jonathan could think of nothing else to do but pray. He called the group of missionaries together in the little room overlooking the meeting hall. "Our home church has failed us," he told them with tears in his eyes, "but the God of Hudson Taylor is ours. He will not fail us if we look to Him. This field must be evangelized, and it cannot be done with our present small force. If we cannot get Canadians as channels for the gospel message, we must get Chinese people instead."

Even as Jonathan was speaking these words, a plan was coming to him. His old friend, Dr. Hayes, ran a Bible college in North China. Jonathan wondered whether Dr. Hayes could spare any workers. He wrote a letter immediately to inquire. Two days later a letter arrived from Dr. Hayes, obviously sent before he'd had time to receive and read Jonathan's urgent request.

Jonathan tore the letter open. Dr. Hayes wrote that all openly Christian work in his area had to be stopped because of the political turmoil. He had an entire graduating class of sixty people who had nowhere to go, and he asked, "Could you use any of these men?"

"Rosalind, come and listen to this!" exclaimed Jonathan, chuckling out loud. "God has supplied our need."

"How many of them will you ask for?" asked Rosalind, looking as pleased as Jonathan did at the swift answer to their prayers.

"I'm going to tell him to send them all," replied Jonathan.

"But..." stammered his wife, turning pale, "Jonathan, where is the money going to come from for their food and lodging? We don't have enough money to support more than five at the most."

Jonathan shook his head. "Have faith," he said. "If God sends us these men, don't you think He will send the money to provide for them, too?"

Rosalind said no more, and Jonathan hurried off to reply to Dr. Hayes. Over the next few weeks, every time the Goforths received mail there were checks in it. Rosalind and the others were amazed at how the money kept pouring in, especially since they had told no one about their new plan. Jonathan was not surprised, however. He knew there would be enough money to cover the new workers' expenses, and so there was. When the sixty new workers arrived a month later, there was enough money to pay their salary for two months. Jonathan saw this as God's seal of approval on their work, and he immediately wrote to Dr. Hayes asking him to find more students who were willing to come to work with them in Manchuria.

Everyone was put to work as soon as he arrived, and there was always enough money to pay the workers their salaries on time.

Winter came, and with it a plague that killed a third of the people in the area. More than ever in the face of this tragedy, the people of Manchuria wanted to hear about God and His love for them. During winter, the location of the meeting hall proved to be more valuable than ever because Jonathan made a point of keeping a roaring fire going in the hall. Hundreds of near-freezing people would stop in on their way along the busy street to sit and rest and talk by the fire. As they warmed themselves, many hundreds of people heard the gospel for the first time.

By the next spring, everything in Szepingkai was going smoothly. Nancy Graham was a fiery preacher whose Salvation Army training had made her bold enough to preach to a room filled with men. Annie Kok, on the other hand, worked well preaching to the women, while the Chinese workers Dr. Hayes had sent worked tirelessly visiting people in their homes and taking turns preaching in the meeting hall.

Sixty-nine-year-old Jonathan Goforth was ready for a new challenge. It was time to move on! He set his sights on Taonan, the next large town farther on up the railway. Allan Reoch went with him, and in the spring of 1928, they started to develop another church in an area where the gospel had never been preached.

Once again they had to rent a building to serve as both a meeting hall and living quarters. This time, though, there was even more work to do before they could begin services. Jonathan and Allan were aghast when they discovered that the landlord had ripped out every wooden fixture from the interior of the building they had rented. The windows, frames, and sills were gone, along with all of the doors. When Jonathan asked the landlord why he had taken everything, he was told that this was the custom when renting a building in Taonan. Every new renter supplied his own doors and windows. It was one more thing to do before the meeting hall was ready.

Eventually everything was done. New windows and doors had been installed, and chairs had been brought in and arranged in the large room. The meeting hall opened for services, and within days, crowds were gathering to hear Jonathan and Allan take turns preaching. In only two weeks, four hundred people had become Christian converts. Jonathan immediately sent to Szepingkai for some workers to come to help disciple the new converts.

One evening, as he sat on a broken chair by the stove, Jonathan was overcome as he thought about the wonderful life he was leading. He turned to Rosalind and said, "Isn't it grand to be out here opening up such a place to the gospel. I'd rather be right here than in Windsor Castle." This was the kind of contagious enthusiasm that inspired all those who worked with him.

The new mission center in Taonan had been open only a month when word came from Nancy Graham that she was going to leave Szepingkai and set up a new mission station at Tungliao. This left Jonathan in a difficult position. He respected Nancy's right to work where she felt called, but the Szepingkai mission was a large one and needed a strong leader. Since Annie Kok was not ready or able to take over the men's side of the work, Jonathan reluctantly made plans to move back to Szepingkai. He left Allan Reoch in charge of the flood of new believers at the Taonan mission church.

The Goforths arrived back in Szepingkai just in time for a brutal winter. They moved into the rooms above the meeting hall, but the only room with a fireplace was their bedroom. As a result, Jonathan was forced to store everything perishable—eggs, apples, canned milk, and potatoes—under their bed so that it would not freeze. Even with a blazing fire roaring in the fireplace, often in the morning Jonathan had to crack the ice that had formed on the top of the water jug.

As the winter progressed, Jonathan began having trouble with his teeth, and in December 1928, he had them all extracted. The operation did not go as well as hoped, and an infection developed in his lower jaw. Jonathan was in so much pain that he was unable to climb down the stairs from his room for four months.

About this time, the Goforths' youngest child, Fred, arrived from Canada with a typewriter. He had often thought his father should record some of his missionary stories, and he arrived intending to do just that. Every morning father and son would go back through Jonathan's old journals and talk about his early missionary experiences in China. By the time Fred left four months later, he had a complete manuscript to take with him. The manuscript became the book *By My Spirit* and was published the following year.

Soon it was time for Jonathan and Rosalind to take another furlough in Canada. They might have chosen to stay in Manchuria except that Rosalind was beginning to lose her sight and she needed to see a specialist. They left behind them a thriving work with thirty evangelists and church workers who were supported by a continuing supply of donations.

On furlough, as the Goforths traveled around Canada and the eastern United States speaking about their work in Manchuria, Jonathan also began to have difficulties with his eyesight. A doctor examined him and diagnosed his condition as a detached retina in his right eye. Several operations were performed in an attempt to reattach the retina, but none of them worked. The surgeon eventually told Jonathan that he would never see out of that eye again. Rosalind's eye operation, on the other hand, was a complete success, and soon she was seeing as well as before.

Once again, Jonathan used his illness as an opportunity to dictate a book. This time Margaret Gay, a nurse and former missionary in Honan province, typed up his account, which became the popular selling book *Miracle Lives of China.*

In 1931, Jonathan and Rosalind Goforth set out for the mission field yet again. The two of them stood on the aft deck of the ship and watched the Olympic Mountains of Washington state slip from view. Both of them thought they were seeing North America for the last time. They were committed to spending their last years on the mission field.

The Goforths continued to work in Manchuria and "vacationed" in Changte. On these vacations, Jonathan would preach at four meetings a day for a week, and each meeting attracted between eight hundred and a thousand people. While in Changte, Jonathan and Rosalind also visited the graves of the three little children they had buried thirty years before. After the death of Constance in October 1902 and Rosalind's subsequent prayer committing herself and her children into God's care, not one of their other children had died. As they stood beside the three small graves, Jonathan did not know it, but it would be the last time he would see them. He was about to go completely blind.

In March 1933, Jonathan felt a strange sensation in his left eye, followed by darkness. Rosalind took him to the best doctor in Peking, who concluded that the retina in Jonathan's left eye had detached, just as the one in his right eye had done two years before. Various surgical operations were performed, but nothing worked, and Jonathan Goforth never saw again.

For a brief few days Jonathan thought his years of ministry were over. He could no longer read or write or see the expressions on the faces of the people he was talking to. But as the finality of his blindness settled over him, he began to discover all the things he could still do. He had read the entire Bible through seventy-three times during his life, and he knew most of the New Testament by heart, in both English and Mandarin. When Chinese Christians came to him, he listened carefully to their concerns and from memory was able to give them the right verse, parable, or story from the Bible to help them with their problem. He could still pray, and he could dictate letters to his fellow workers in the outlying areas of Manchuria. When Jonathan Goforth eventually left Peking to return to Manchuria, his mind was made up. Blindness might cause him a few minor difficulties, but it would not stop him from completing the work he still had to do.

Chapter 15

Faithful Servant of Jesus Christ

The situation was tenser than ever when the Goforths returned to Manchuria. By now the Japanese had created a puppet state there, and they were busy promoting their own interests. Gangs of bandits roamed the countryside looking for victims. Sometimes there were up to a thousand bandits in these gangs, which would often take over entire towns and villages, looting and vandalizing everything. The bandits hated anything to do with the foreign powers, including the Christian religion. They took special delight in murdering Chinese Christians and burning down churches. Still, Jonathan was grateful that despite the persecution, most Christians held firm.

Many stories were relayed to Jonathan about the bravery of Christians in the face of these bandits. The story that thrilled him the most was that of the Sun girls. Sun Wen and Sun Guang were cousins, aged twelve and fourteen. Their family belonged to the church in Fanchiatun, north of Szepingkai. When Jonathan paid one of his many visits there, Sun Wen told him about her encounter with the bandits.

"Three weeks ago," Sun Wen began, "my mother yelled that there were bandits at the front gate. Everyone panicked and ran out of the house, escaping through the back courtyard, except for my cousin Guang. I was looking for her when the bandits began battering down the door. Just then my cousin yelled that she was in the storage room, but it was too late for me to run to her. So I just knelt down on the floor and began to pray. When the door burst open, about twenty men rushed in. The leader of the gang grabbed me by the throat and said, 'Tell me where your father is, girl, or I will kill you.' 'I don't know,' I said, and I didn't. I had no idea in which direction my family had fled."

When Sun Wen stopped to catch her breath, Jonathan leaned in to hear the rest of her story.

"Anyway," she went on, "this made the bandit very angry, and he started squeezing my throat more tightly, yelling, 'You're lying. You're lying.' 'No,' I told him, 'I am a Christian.' Then I had a strange idea. I felt that I should offer to sing to the leader, so I said, 'I think you would enjoy my singing.' The bandit looked at me strangely, and then he took his hands off my throat and stood back. I began singing, 'Jesus loves me, this I know, for the Bible tells me so…' At first no one paid much attention to me. The bandits were running around piling up all the valuables in the house, ready to load them into their carts. But one by one they stopped to listen. When I was finished, several of them yelled, 'More, sing us more!' Then I thought of Guang hiding in the other room. I had an idea, 'Oh, I love to sing,' I said, 'but my cousin is in the other room, and she sings much better than me. I will call her, and we will sing to you together.' I called Guang, and she came out of her hiding place. We began to sing the second verse of the chorus. When we were finished, the head bandit said, 'We must stop looting now and put everything back the way it was.' Then he began dragging a large urn back against the wall. Before he left, do you know what he did?" Sun Wen asked Jonathan.

"No," he replied. "Tell me."

"He pulled some money from his pocket and gave Guang and me a dollar each."

"Weren't you scared when you were surrounded by the bandits?" Jonathan asked.

"Oh no!" exclaimed Sun Wen. "I knew the Lord Jesus was with me."

Jonathan wondered how many Christians in Canada would have displayed the same kind of faith as Sun Wen in the face of such a terrifying situation.

Despite the encouraging reports that Jonathan and Allan Reoch forwarded to Canada, the

Presbyterian Foreign Missions Board sent word in June 1933 that it was going to drastically cut funding for the work in Manchuria. Europe and North America were in the midst of the Great Depression, and there was simply not enough money to send to missionaries. At first Jonathan was troubled by the board's decision. He feared he would be forced to dismiss many of the seventy full-time Chinese and Manchurian workers who served with the mission. He worried about the impact this would have on the forty new churches that had sprung up around the region.

Jonathan need not have worried, because an interesting thing began to happen. As he told the Manchurian Christians that their pastors and workers might lose their jobs, the churches themselves rose up to take on the financial responsibility for their workers. Even though the Canadian churches stopped supporting them, not a single worker had to leave because of lack of funds. It was an amazing responsibility for such new churches. In 1932, the Manchurian churches had given $4,312 towards their own missionaries' salaries and the general running of their churches. By the end of 1934, this amount had risen to $14,065! Baptisms were up, too. In 1932, 472 adults were baptized, and by late 1934, the number had grown to 966. By all accounts, the churches in Manchuria were thriving.

Jonathan's health, though, was not doing so well. Jonathan insisted on continuing to hold meetings all over Manchuria. The local people flocked to hear him. They eagerly asked him questions, and together they discussed the meaning of passages from the Bible. Jonathan never complained to any of them, not even his wife, about his blindness. He also came close to death several times in 1934, first from a bout of the flu and then from pneumonia. Still, he would not consider giving up his post, at least not until three things happened that caused him to reconsider.

First, Jonathan received a letter from a well-known Presbyterian pastor in Toronto urging him to consider returning to Canada. Jonathan churned the words over in his mind. "I very well understand that you will feel that you ought to stay at the post of duty up to the very end—but have you ever thought that God may be demanding the greater sacrifice of your coming home and, out of your ripe experience, rekindling the fires of missionary zeal that are, I assure you, on the decline in the Home Church."

Jonathan had not thought of going home, and the letter itself did not persuade him to do so. There was still plenty of work to be done in Manchuria. However, a second letter arrived from another prominent Canadian pastor, also urging Jonathan to consider coming home. Again it was not enough to sway him. Then Rosalind became very ill, and the local doctor told Jonathan that she would die without special medical help. Finally, Jonathan Goforth knew it was time to move back to his homeland.

The farewell to all their friends and coworkers was long and drawn-out. Thousands of people from the forty-eight churches that Jonathan had helped start in Manchuria came to catch one last glimpse of their beloved pastor. Jonathan could not see the dazzling array of hand-embroidered silk, satin, and velvet banners that decorated the Szepingkai church. Tears rolled down his cheeks as Rosalind described each one to him in great detail. The banners were emblazoned with messages such as "A True Pastor Leaves Love Behind" and "Faithful Servant of Jesus Christ."

When the time finally arrived for the train to depart, it was almost too much for Jonathan to bear. Rosalind stood him at the carriage window and described the scene to him. A sea of Manchurian Christians, many of them converted as a direct result of Jonathan's preaching, stood hoping for one last glimpse of the man they loved so dearly. Although the windows were shut and the crowd was huge, Jonathan wanted some way to communicate to them one last time just how much he loved them. He bowed his head and touched his heart, and then he lifted his face upward, as if he were looking to heaven, where they would one day all be together again. As he did this, the entire crowd burst out weeping and continued to weep as the train chugged away from the station.

On his return home, Jonathan Goforth was in great demand as a speaker throughout Canada and the United States. With Rosalind, her health now improving, at his side he spoke an average of ten times a week, both in small churches and at large interdenominational gatherings. His message was always the same: The door is open and more people are needed to carry the gospel to the ends of the earth. Jonathan challenged everyone who listened to him with the question "Why can't you go?" It was the same question that had challenged him over fifty years before when he sat listening to Dr. Mackay describe the opportunities that existed and the need for more workers in Formosa. The challenge had ultimately led Jonathan to the mission field and a life of fruitful service there. Now he hoped his question would challenge other young people to go.

October 7, 1936, was like so many other days in Jonathan Goforth's life. He spoke at a church service that was about forty miles away from where he was staying and arrived home late that night. He was exhausted but glad to have been able to speak to so many people. He climbed into bed and fell quickly into a deep sleep from which he would never wake up. His heart stopped beating sometime in the early hours of the next morning. He was seventy-seven years old.

Jonathan Goforth's funeral service was held at Knox Church in Toronto, where forty-nine years before he had stood at the same altar and dedicated his life for service in China. Seldom had the church seen such a large funeral service. Speaker after speaker spoke of the great work Jonathan had done. They also reminded the gathered crowd of his generosity, love, and grateful attitude, something that even blindness could not rob him of. Jonathan had seen an open door for missionary service in China, and he had walked through it. In the process he became one of China's greatest evangelists, leaving behind as his legacy many thousands of Chinese Christians.

Bibliography

Goforth, Rosalind. *Jonathan Goforth.* Bethany House, 1986.

Goforth, Rosalind. *Climbing: Memories of a Missionary's Wife.* Bethel Publishing, 1998.

Goforth, Jonathan and Rosalind Goforth. *Miracle Lives of China.* Zondervan, 1931.

About the Authors

Janet and Geoff Benge are a husband and wife writing team with more than thirty years of writing experience. Janet is a former elementary school teacher. Geoff holds a degree in history. Originally from New Zealand, the Benges spent ten years serving with Youth With A Mission. They have two daughters, Laura and Shannon, and an adopted son, Lito. They make their home in the Orlando, Florida, area.